Tolley'
Guide to Self-Assessment for the Self-Employed

Second Edition

by

Peter Gravestock FCA FTII ATT

Tolley Publishing Company Limited

un A United Newspapers publication

Published by
Tolley Publishing Company Ltd
Tolley House
2 Addiscombe Road
Croydon, Surrey CR9 5AF England
0181-686 9141

Printed and bound in Great Britain by
Hobbs the Printers, Southampton

© Tolley Publishing Company Ltd 1995

ISBN 1 86012032-6

Preface

The reform of the personal taxation system in this country, by a gradual move to a system of self-assessment and a current year basis of assessment, has been discussed for a number of years. The first document forming the consultation process for the current changes was published in 1991.

The Finance Act 1994 introduced the first (albeit the major) tranche of legislation which, when completed, will encompass the whole personal taxation system, including employees as well as the self-employed.

The process has continued with the additional legislation contained in the Finance Act 1995, and further legislation must be expected as consultation takes place on the effect of these reforms on the taxpayer and the Revenue.

The result of these changes will be a complete change of emphasis such that the responsibility for all day to day actions relating to personal taxation falls upon the taxpayer, and the enforcement powers of the taxation authorities are significantly increased.

I would like to thank Richard Hill for his invaluable help, assistance and encouragement in the preparation of this book.

Peter Gravestock, FCA FTII ATT
Gravestock and Owen
Willenhall
West Midlands
May 1995

Contents

	Page
Preface	iii
1. Introduction	1
2. Self-Assessment	4
The present procedure	4
Self-assessment	4
Administration	5
Payment dates	5
Enforcement	6
Corrections to returns	6
Enquiries into a return	6
Determination of tax where no return delivered	7
Discovery	7
Tax district	7
Time limits	7
Tax returns	7
Filing dates	8
Notification of sources of income	8
Records	9
Partnership returns	10
Partnership statement	11
Amendments to partnership statement	12
Enquiries into partnership return	12
Trustees' returns	12
Enquiries into tax returns	12
Notification of an enquiry	13
Power to call for documents	14
Amendments whilst enquiry continues	14
Conclusion of enquiry	14
Payment of tax	15
3. The Penalty Regime	19
Enforcement	19
Interest	19
Amendments to tax returns	20
Appeals	20
Interest on overdue tax	20
Interest on interim payments where eventual liability exceeds preceding year liability	20
Interest remitted where eventual liability is lower than interim payment	22
Surcharges	23

	A worked example of interest and surcharge	23
	Assessments and determinations	24
	Determination of tax where no return delivered	24
	Assessment where a loss of tax is discovered	25
	Penalty for late filing of tax return	26
	Notification of chargeability	26
	Keeping of records	27
	Production of documents	27
	Interest on penalties	27
	Claims	27
	Error or mistake claims	28
	Assessments for 1995/96 and earlier years	28
4.	**Payments of Tax for 1996/97**	29
	Payments on account in 1996/97	29
	Higher rate liability	29
	Schedule A and Schedule D Cases III to VI	30
	Schedule D Cases I and II	30
	Reductions of payment on account	30
	Computation of amount payable in 1996/97	30
	Example – Schedule D Case I income only	31
	Example with investment income	32
	Partnerships	34
5.	**Current Year Basis of Assessment**	35
	Preceding year basis – the reasons for change	35
	Dealing with the Revenue under the old system	36
	Current year basis – the concepts	38
	The new rules	38
	Dealings with the Revenue under the new system	39
6.	**Opening and Closing Years**	41
	New principles	41
	Overlap relief	41
	Capital allowances and losses	41
	Apportionments	42
	Use of 31 March as year end	42
	Opening years	42
	Accounts prepared to 5 April	42
	Accounts prepared to a date other than 5 April	43
	Short life businesses	43
	A business that makes up its accounts to a date twelve months after the date of commencement	44
	First accounts ending in fiscal year of commencement	44
	First accounts for more than twelve months ending in second year of assessment	45

Contents

First accounts ending in the third year of assessment	46
First accounts for less than twelve months ending in second year of assessment	47
Commencement of new rules	49
Summary of the opening year rules	49
Closing years	49
Overlap relief	49
Accounting date of 5 April	49
Accounting date of other than 5 April	50
More than one accounting date in year of cessation	50
No accounting date in penultimate year of assessment	52
Existing businesses ceasing	53
Example of cessation after 6 April 1999	54
Example of cessation in 1998/99	55
Example of cessation in 1997/98	55

7. Transitional Rules for Existing Businesses — 57

Existing businesses	57
The fiscal year 1996/97	57
Overlap relief on transition	57
Example of transitional year without change of accounting date	58
Change of accounting date in the transitional period	58
Example of transitional year with change of accounting date	59
Anti-avoidance	60
Should you change your accounting date to 5 April?	61
Example of rising profits	62
Example of declining profits	63
Businesses not on PY basis for 1995/96	63

8. Capital Allowances — 66

The changes	66
Deduction as a trading expense	66
Period of account	66
Claims for capital allowances	67
Notification of expenditure	67
Introduction of new rules	67
A worked example	68

9. Change of Accounting Date — 72

The objectives of the legislation	72
A period of account of less than twelve months ending in the next fiscal year	72
A period of account of less than twelve months ending in the same fiscal year	72

A period of account of more than twelve months ending in the next fiscal year	72
A period of account of more than twelve months such that there is a fiscal year without accounts	73
Conditions for change of accounting date	73
Examples of change of accounting date	74
A period of account of less than twelve months ending in the next fiscal year	74
A period of account of less than twelve months ending in the same fiscal year	75
A period of account of more than twelve months ending in the next fiscal year	76
A period of account of more than twelve months such that there is a fiscal year without accounts	76
Accounts for more than 18 months	78
Failure to give notice	79

10. Partnerships — 80

Self-assessment with partnership income	80
New partners	81
Retirement of a partner	83
The continuing partners	83
Change of partner before 5 April 1997	84
The transitional period	84
Current year basis – a worked example	85
Partnerships assessed on an actual basis in 1995/96	89
Corporate partners	90
Income other than Schedule D I/II	91

11. Losses — 92

Fiscal year basis in practice	92
Loss relief under current year basis	92
Relief for trading losses against other income	93
Relief for trading losses in opening years	95
Relief for national insurance	98
Relief for trading losses carried forward	98
Relief for terminal losses	100
Restriction of relief in respect of farming and market gardening	103
Relief for losses on unquoted shares	103
Loss relief in 1996/97	103

12. Other Changes — 106

Principles of self-assessment	106
Schedule D Case III	106
Example of a continuing source	107
Example of a source closing before 5 April 1998	107

Contents

Example of a new source	107
Schedule D Cases IV and V	108
Summary of basis of assessment	108
Remittance basis	109
Schedule D Case VI	109
Lloyd's underwriters	110
Double taxation relief in respect of overlap profits	110
Farmers' averaging provisions	111
Schedule E	111
Capital gains	112
Future legislation	112

Chapter 1

Introduction

1.1 Income tax was originally introduced by Pitt. This was in the Budget speech on 3 December 1798, a speech that lasted an hour. The measure was unpopular and yielded a very small amount of money, under £6 million in the first year. Thus in April 1802 Addington repealed the original income tax.

The abolition lasted as long as the peace with France and when hostilities recommenced in May 1803 the Budget of that year introduced what was called 'a separate tax on property'. Although passed under the title *Property Duty Act*, it was in fact income tax in another form and laid the foundations of the Schedule system. Many of the basic principles established in those early years are still with us today.

1.2 The preceding basis of assessment for the self-employed was introduced by Winston Churchill in 1926. On many occasions since that time attempts have been made to change the basis of assessment applied to the profits of the self-employed and certain other income, from preceding year basis to current year basis, without success.

The increasing numbers of self-employed, rising from under two million in 1979 to over four million in 1994, together with changing work patterns and the anticipated growth in home working, has put the preceding year basis of assessment under strain. Although the rules are well known to taxation advisors, they often remain a complete mystery to many clients.

With the growth of the number of self-employed persons, the percentage of those taxpayers using professional advisors has declined, such that the Inland Revenue finds that it has to compute the assessments in many instances. It is estimated that approximately one half of the self-employed do not have professional advisors.

1.3 With the increased pressure upon the Government to be more efficient, it has not gone unnoticed that in the USA the same number of revenue offices collect many times the amount of tax collected in the UK from three times as many people.

The administrative costs of the Revenue computing and issuing assessments is compounded by the failure of the average taxpayer to submit accounts timeously. As a result many assessments are issued in estimated figures against which the

1.4 Introduction

taxpayer must appeal. Of those appeals, a significant number are listed for hearing before the General Commissioners and are no more than delay hearings.

1.4 Parliament has therefore decided to undertake a radical restructuring of the UK taxation system for individuals and partnerships. The onus upon assessing the taxpayer moves from the Revenue to self-assessment. As with all self-assessment systems, this will be backed by an effective penalty regime and will be monitored by the Revenue, with powers of random audit known as 'enquiry'.

Because self-assessment requires an understanding of the basis of assessment by the taxpayer, it is felt that the present system of assessment, based upon profits arising in a preceding year, should be replaced by a simpler system.

The original consultation proposals did offer simple solutions, but unfortunately those proposals would have led to inequity in many instances. After lengthy consultation, the *Finance Act 1994* introduces legislation that is fair, but not necessarily simple.

It is clear that the legislator required a system that significantly reduced the possibility of tax avoidance. This is done by ensuring that the profits that will be taxed for any business, or for any other source, will exactly equal the amount earned. By contrast, the preceding year basis of assessment for the self-employed could result in greater, or lesser, profits being assessed over the life of the business than those earned.

In drafting the new legislation care has been taken to ensure that, within reason, a taxpayer can choose whichever accounting date he or she wishes, and that he can change that accounting date at any time, giving maximum consideration to commercial requirements.

A final problem was that in the UK, traditionally, not all taxpayers have been required to submit a tax return. To incorporate proposals that every taxpayer must submit a tax return each year would significantly increase the Revenue collection costs. The reason that the UK can manage without tax returns from all taxpayers is that a significant proportion of the tax yield is collected by way of PAYE from employed persons and by deduction at source. These provisions are to continue substantially unaltered. However, under self-assessment it will be necessary for the taxpayer to notify new sources of income and liability to higher rate tax at an earlier stage.

1.5 The UK tax system will change to a self-assessed basis with effect from 1996/97. If the taxpayer wishes the Revenue to assist with the assessment procedure, then this will be possible providing the taxpayer submits his or her tax return at an early stage. The change will be accompanied by a move from the preceding year basis of assessment to a current year basis. This will be achieved in 1997/98, with a transitional year in 1996/97.

As a result of the above changes, the current concept of taxing partnerships, with a joint and several liability to each partner, changes from 1997/98 to self-assessment upon the individual partners. The partnership will continue to submit a return, together with a statement dividing income from all sources between the partners in their profit-sharing ratio of the period of account. The individual partner will be responsible for computing his own self-assessment and for paying his own tax.

The current year basis of assessment will apply to all new businesses commencing on or after 6 April 1994.

1.6 The above measures are considered in detail in the following chapters. As this is a completely new system, it must be expected that further legislation will be required. A number of measures have been introduced by the *Finance Act 1995*, and it must be expected that there will be similar legislative changes introduced in the *Finance Act 1996*. It will also be possible for such changes to be introduced in the *Finance Act 1997*. Care should be taken to incorporate such later legislation into the measures described in this book.

Chapter 2

Self-Assessment

The present procedure

2.1 The UK tax system has been based upon the premise that the Inland Revenue assesses the taxpayer. There is an obligation for the taxpayer to report to the Revenue sources of income, and the Revenue will normally issue a tax return on which the quantum of the income can be declared to the Revenue source by source. Having received such information, the Revenue will assess the taxpayer. It is the duty of the Inspector to raise the assessment based upon the details of income provided to him, but if it appears to him that the return is incomplete or incorrect or has not be made, then he may assess income to tax to the best of his judgment.

Income in the UK is computed for taxation purposes by reference to the Schedular System. The relevant tax office issues assessments for income source by source, the tax return being submitted to the taxpayer's main taxing district which coordinates the issuing of assessments and the granting of allowances. If the Revenue does not make an assessment on returned income then there is no liability to tax. When an assessment is made, the taxpayer may appeal against the assessment and the final assessable profits will be determined by agreement, pending appeal, or by the appeals procedure.

If the Revenue has raised an assessment which the taxpayer believes to be excessive, then the remedy is to appeal. At that time it is possible to make a separate postponement application to hold-over the tax believed to be excessive. If such a postponement application is accepted by the Revenue, then the taxpayer is only obliged to pay the agreed reduced tax, and interest, if any, will only be charged on the balance of the tax liability.

Once an assessment has been agreed it cannot be changed. However, the taxpayer may make an error or mistake claim if he discovers that the assessment is incorrect. The Revenue may issue a further assessment if the Inspector discovers that profits have not been assessed, or that the assessment has become insufficient. The assessment cannot be amended merely because the Inspector of Taxes has failed to act upon information available to him (*Scorer v Olin Energy Systems Limited 1985 STC 218*).

Self-assessment

2.2 The long-established and well-known principles of assessment and appeal, together with the Inland Revenue practice of in-depth enquiry into accounts of traders, will be completely changed from 1996/97.

A taxpayer will be required to file his tax return by 31 January following the end of the fiscal year. The return will be in many parts. The 'tax return' itself will contain a summary of income, capital gains, charges, and allowances. All items will be shown for the actual fiscal year in question, or on a current year basis. The return will compute the tax liability for the year of assessment, and the amounts payable on 31 January following the end of the fiscal year (or tax repayable).

2.3 If the taxpayer wishes the Revenue to compute his tax liability, then he need not complete that part of the return. In those circumstances the return must be filed by 30 September following the year of assessment. Although the Revenue may be requested to compute the tax liability, they are undertaking the task effectively as agents for the taxpayer, and the resultant assessment is still known as a self-assessment.

Accordingly the onus of assessment moves from the Inland Revenue to the taxpayer.

Administration

Payment dates

2.4 As a consequence of the new tax return and self-assessment provisions, the date of payment of income tax and capital gains tax alters. In the case of capital gains tax, the liability becomes due on 31 January following the end of the year of assessment.

For income tax, interim payments will normally be required. The actual tax liability of the preceding year will be used as the basis of the interim payment. The liability for this purpose is the amount assessed in the preceding year, less amounts deducted at source, notional tax credits, tax credits and deductions under PAYE. There is no adjustment for changing levels of income or tax rates and allowances.

2.5 This change means that effectively higher rate liability on investment income becomes payable as to:

(a) one half on 31 January during the tax year; and
(b) one half on 31 July following,

rather than on 1 December following the end of the tax year.

2.6 The interim payments will be 50% of the relevant figure payable on 31 January in the year of assessment, together with 50% of the relevant amount payable on 31 July following the end of the year of assessment.

When the actual tax liability for the year is computed, the balance of the tax

2.7 Self-Assessment

payable, or repayable, will be due on 31 January following the end of the year of assessment.

There will be provisions to enable the taxpayer to reduce the interim payments if he believes that his liability for the current year will be less than in the preceding year.

Interest will be charged on all late payments and repayment interest will be paid on any overpayments from the due date or the date of payment if later.

For further details see 2.25 below.

Enforcement

2.7 There will be automatic penalties for failure to file a tax return by the due date. Furthermore, any tax unpaid 28 days after the filing date for the tax return will be subject to a surcharge of 5%. That surcharge increases to 10% if tax is unpaid six months after the relevant filing date. See paragraph 3.8.

Corrections to returns

2.8 Where a taxpayer does not have full information by the relevant filing date, he will be required to make a best estimate. Tax will be due on that estimate. When the information is available to complete the return, interest will be charged on the tax due from the normal due date to the date of payment, or repayment interest paid on the tax repayable, from the due date (or date of payment if later) to the date of repayment. Surcharges and penalties will not apply.

A taxpayer will be able to correct his tax return at any time in the period of twelve months from the normal filing date. The Revenue will be able to correct a tax return for obvious errors in a period of nine months from the date on which the return is actually filed. This process will be known as 'repairing' a tax return [new *TMA 1970, ss 9, 12AB*].

Enquiries into a return

2.9 The Revenue will have the power to enquire into any tax return. This power is extended to corporation tax returns. If the Revenue wishes to exercise this power they must give notice in writing within one year of the filing date. This period is extended if the taxpayer is late in filing his tax return. After such a notice has been given, it will not be possible to repair a tax return.

The Revenue will be required to issue a formal notice when they have completed their enquiries. If a taxpayer believes that an enquiry should not have been undertaken, or is being continued unreasonably, he can ask the General Commissioners to issue a notice requiring the Revenue to close the enquiries. When the Revenue has completed its enquiries, it must issue a formal notice to the taxpayer. After such a notice has been issued, it will not be possible for the Revenue to conduct further enquiries into that tax return, unless there is a discovery.

Determination of tax where no return delivered

2.10 If a taxpayer does not file his tax return then the Revenue will have powers to issue a determination. The tax shown on such a determination will be payable without appeal and no postponement of tax will be possible. The determination will be superseded when the tax return and self-assessment are filed. See paragraph 3.12.

Discovery

2.11 The legislation introduces provisions relating to discovery. In simple terms, a discovery assessment will only be possible if there has been fraud, negligent conduct or inadequate disclosure by the taxpayer. See paragraph 3.14.

Tax district

2.12 Under the new system, each taxpayer will have only one tax district and one tax reference. Having arrived at the quantum of the assessable income by using the Schedular System, all income will be aggregated, less charges and allowances, to arrive at one liability. The taxpayer will file his self-assessment at his tax district and pay to the relevant tax accounts office.

Time limits

2.13 Most time limits will be changed to bring them in line with the new filing date of 31 January following the year of assessment [*TMA 1970, s 43(1)* as amended]. The new general time limit will therefore become five years from 31 January following the year of assessment, i.e. for 1997/98 the filing date will be 31 January 1999 with the normal time limit for claims being 31 January 2004 (as opposed to 5 April 2004 under the old system). Many claims will have a time limit of one year after normal filing date, i.e. 31 January 2000 in the above example. In the case of fraud or negligent conduct, the latest date for assessment will be 20 years from 31 January following the tax year, i.e. the 31 January 2019 for 1997/98. When a taxpayer dies, assessments must be issued within three years of 31 January following the fiscal year of death i.e. for a death on 6 May 1997 (1997/98), the latest date is 31 January 2002.

Tax returns

2.14 The new-style tax returns will deal only with one fiscal year. All details shown thereon will relate to the same period. This contrasts to the present tax return, where income is shown for the current year and allowances for the following year.

Tax returns will not be issued automatically to all taxpayers. As at present, returns will be issued to all taxpayers who are known to require a tax return, i.e. anyone who is self-employed, has a higher rate tax liability or who is likely to be a special case, e.g. directors, pensioners, or those likely to receive a tax repayment.

2.15 Self-Assessment

The working draft issued by the Revenue indicates that the new returns will consist of a summary form together with schedules for each source of income, allowance or adjustment. The taxpayer will only submit such schedules as are required for his individual circumstances. Sub-schedules known as 'Help Sheets' will be provided where appropriate.

The draft currently provides for fifteen schedules for income and gains and three other schedules to back the return. Although it is unlikely that any taxpayer will have to complete all the schedules, a separate form will be required for each employment or self-employment.

Each taxpayer for whom a return is required will be sent a tax return form and guide, together with schedules required based upon the income reported on the previous tax return and notified new sources. Any additional schedules or help sheets required will be provided on request.

Filing dates

2.15 Where a return is issued in the normal way, the taxpayer will be required to file the tax return by 31 January following the end of the tax year [new *TMA 1970, s 8(1A)(a)* substituted by *FA 1994, s 178(1)*]. There will be an automatic penalty for failure to meet that deadline.

Where a return is issued after 31 October then the normal filing date will be three months from the date on which the return is issued [*s 8(1A)(b)*].

If a taxpayer does not wish to work out his own tax liability then the return must be filed by 30 September. If the return is issued after 31 July then the return must be filed within two months of the date of issue, if the Revenue are to compute the self-assessment [new *TMA 1970, s 9(2)* substituted by *FA 1994, s 179*].

If a taxpayer submits a tax return without self-assessment after the dates mentioned above, i.e. 30 September or two months after the date of issue, then the Revenue will attempt to assess the taxpayer by the due date for payment. If they fail to issue an assessment by that time, then interest will run from the normal due date of payment, notwithstanding that the taxpayer will not know his liability at that time because the Revenue has been unable to quantify the liability speedily.

Notification of sources of income

2.16 To ensure that the Revenue issues tax returns to all relevant taxpayers, the period of time for notification of new sources of income is reduced to six months from the end of the relevant year of assessment, i.e. for income sources arising in 1996/97 notification will be due by 6 October 1997 [new *TMA 1970, s 7* substituted by *FA 1994, 19 Sch 1*].

The above requirement is not applied where there are no chargeable gains and income is subject to deduction of tax at source to meet the liability. There is therefore a liability to notify to the Revenue by 5 October following the end of the year if a higher rate liability arises due to the receipt of investment income taxed at source. In the same way a liability to notify arises if untaxed interest is received.

It should be noted that this new notification period applies for the tax year 1995/96 onwards.

2.17 If the taxpayer fails to notify the Revenue by 5 October following the end of a fiscal year, then he will be liable to a penalty not exceeding the net tax unpaid by 31 January following the year of assessment.

Example

2.18 John commenced self-employment on 1 June 1996. He did not give notice of chargeability for the year 1996/97 by 5 October 1997. His accountant gave notice to the Revenue on 12 December 1997. John paid £2,000 on account of his tax liability on 30 January 1998. His eventual liability for that year was £4,200. John will be liable to a penalty of an amount not exceeding £2,200. See also paragraph 3.18 below.

2.19 It should be noted that it is quite possible that notification of a source will be required before the first accounting date, e.g. Jane commenced trading on 1 January 1997 making her accounts up to 31 December 1997. The source will therefore commence in the fiscal year 1996/97 and notification will be required by 5 October 1997. It is quite possible that the professional advisor will not be asked to act until after the end of the first trading year. By that time, the notification date will have passed and in practice it may be that the date for payment, in the above example 31 January 1998, will also have passed. The new client will therefore commence with a tax liability that is increased by interest, surcharges and penalties.

Records

2.20 For the first time, a requirement to keep records for income tax will be introduced into the legislation. This will be *TMA 1970, s 12B* [inserted by *FA 1994, 19 Sch 3*] which applies from 1996/97 onwards.

All taxpayers will be required to retain all records that have been used to complete their tax returns. Such records must be kept until one year after the normal filing date, or, if the return is filed late, one year after the quarter date following the filing date [*s 12B(2)(b)*]. For this purpose the quarter dates are 31 January, 30 April, 31 July and 31 October.

Example

2.21 Joyce files her tax return for 1996/97 on 3 January 1998. The normal filing date is 31 January 1998, therefore records must be maintained until 31 January 1999.

2.22   *Self-Assessment*

Example

2.22   Jason files his tax return for 1996/97 on 2 May 1998. The normal filing date was 31 January 1998, therefore records must be maintained until one year after the quarter date following the date of filing, i.e. date of filing is 2 May 1998, next quarter date is 31 July 1998, records to be maintained until 31 July 1999.

It should be noted that the above dates correspond to the last date that the Revenue can commence enquiries into a tax return. If the Revenue opens an enquiry, then the records must be maintained until the enquiry is completed.

2.23   In the case of a person carrying on a trade, profession or business, or engaged in the letting of property, all tax records must be maintained for five years from 31 January following the year of assessment, e.g. Jacqueline is in business, she must maintain her records for the period of account ending in the fiscal year 1996/97 until five years after 31 January 1998, i.e. until 31 January 2003 [*s 12B(2)(a)*].

The records to be kept by traders include records of all amounts received and expended in the course of trade, including evidence relating to the receipts and expenditure, e.g. all sales and purchase and expense invoices. The records maintained must include supporting documents, i.e. accounts, books, deeds, contract vouchers, receipts, etc. The documents need not be maintained in their original form but they must be in a form that is admissible as evidence [*s 12B(3)(4)*]. Failure to comply with this section will give rise to a penalty not exceeding £3000.

Partnership returns

2.24   The new legislation alters the principles of partnership taxation. The previous concept of joint and several liability of the partners for the tax liability of the partnership is repealed. From 1997/98, for those partnerships that are existing businesses at 5 April 1994, and from 1994/95 for new partnerships (including those treated as new because there is no continuation election), each partner will be liable individually on his share of the profits based upon the allocation in the relevant accounting period.

2.25   However, each partner will not agree his own share of profits with the Revenue. Instead the Revenue will issue a partnership return to an agreed partner [*TMA 1970, s 12AA* inserted by *FA 1994, s 184*]. That partner will agree the assessable profits with the Revenue. Thus the partnership will only deal with one tax office. Having agreed the partnership assessment in respect of income from all sources, and the division of that income between the partners in accordance with the profit-sharing ratio of the accounting period, that information will be passed to the individual partners for inclusion in their own tax returns.

It will not be possible for each partner to agree his separate share of partnership profits, but it will still be possible to have personal expense claims included within the partnership statement to arrive at the tax payable by the partner personally.

2.26 The Revenue will issue a partnership return, which must be filed and include details of:

(a) name, residence and tax reference of each partner;
(b) a division between the partners of the profits from each source;
(c) a partnership statement together with a copy of the accounts and other computations;
(d) details of chargeable assets acquired or disposed of by the partnership; and
(e) a declaration that the return is complete and correct.

If the partnership has not notified the Revenue of the name of the partner to receive the return on behalf of the partnership, then the Revenue may issue a notice to any or all of the partners individually.

The time limit for filing the partnership return will be 31 January following the year of assessment [*s 12AA(4)*], although in practice it will be necessary to file the return before that date, so that the information may be passed to the individual partners for inclusion within their own returns. The normal penalty of £100 for failure to file by the due date (increasing to £200 after six months) will apply to the partnership return as well as to the individual returns with penalties not exceeding £60 per day imposable by the Commissioners. The penalty will be charged on each individual partner for the failure to file the partnership return.

2.27 If the partnership includes a company, the return date will be the later of:

(a) twelve months from the end of the relevant period of account;
(b) three months after the date of issue; or
(c) 31 January following the end of the fiscal year (providing at least one partner is an individual) [*s 12AA(5)*].

Partnership statement

2.28 The return must be accompanied by the accounts and a partnership statement. *TMA 1970, s 12AB* [inserted by *FA 1994, s 185*] requires a statement setting out the amount of income, loss or charge from each source and the share of that income, loss or charge accruing to each partner.

Where the partnership has Schedule D Case I income then the basis of assessment of all income is determined by the accounting date of the trading source. The other income is treated as arising in a second deemed trade, and overlap relief is computed as for a trade (see Chapter 6). However the overlap relief is only useable on a change of accounting date or when the individual ceases to be a partner (not on the cessation of the second deemed trade) [*ICTA 1988, s 111* as introduced by *Finance Act 1995*].

It should be noted that, in the case of an admission of a new partner, it may be that the assessment on the new partner (as an individual) will be based upon a

2.29 *Self-Assessment*

period of account that ends in the following fiscal year. It would not appear that details of estimates of such amounts will be required in the partnership statement. Such an estimate will only be required in the return of the individual.

Amendments to partnership statement

2.29 The legislation includes a power for the partnership to correct its partnership statement at any time up to twelve months after the normal filing date. In the same way, the Revenue may repair the statement in a period of nine months following the date that it is filed with the Revenue [*TMA 1970, s 12AB(2)*].

Enquiries into partnership return

2.30 The Revenue can conduct enquiries into a partnership return in the same way that it can conduct enquiries into the returns of individuals [*TMA 1970, s 12AC* inserted by *FA 1994, s 186*]. If it opens an enquiry into the partnership return then it will be deemed to have commenced an enquiry into the return of each partner, thus preventing amendments to the individual's own return until the enquiry is completed. By comparison, the Revenue can commence an enquiry into the return of an individual partner without opening an enquiry into the return of the partnership. On completion of an enquiry into a partnership, the Revenue must give notice of any amendments to each individual partner to enable them to correct their own self-assessment (see 2.43 below).

Trustees' returns

2.31 The rules relating to individuals set out above will also apply to trustees. They will be required to submit tax returns against the same time limits as individuals, and to self-assess in the same way [*FA 1994, s 178(2)*].

A trustee's return will include a statement showing the amounts in which the beneficiaries or settlor is liable to tax, as well as details of the amount upon which the trustees are liable to tax. As for partnerships, the return may be made by a nominated trustee, or the Revenue may give notice to any or all trustees to make returns. The filing date will be as for individuals. All returns issued must be filed by the due date to avoid penalties.

Enquiries into tax returns

2.32 The previous principle of in-depth enquiries for the self-employed will be replaced by statutory provisions to enquire into a tax return [*TMA 1970, s 9A* inserted by *FA 1994, s 180*]. Because this power is intended to give the Revenue the right to enquire into any tax return, an officer will not have to give a reason for the commencement of an enquiry. However statutory procedures will have to be followed to open and to close an enquiry.

An enquiry can be made into the return of an individual, a trustee, a partnership or a company.

2.33 Enquiry must be distinguished from the Revenue's and taxpayer's rights to repair a tax return. A repair will be the correction by the Revenue of any obvious error or mistake in the return. This can include errors of principle, arithmetical mistakes or other errors. In the case of a taxpayer, it is his or her right to amend the return for any reason. This will include the correction of figures where best estimates have been needed. This will include:

(a) where a business commences and profits are not known by the relevant filing date;
(b) when an individual joins a partnership and the accounting date is such that the following year's accounts are needed to compute the current assessable profits;
(c) profits on cessation, where the individual was a member of a partnership, and the date of cessation means that accounts will be required for a period of account ending in the following fiscal year (see Chapter 10).

2.34 It should be noted that if a taxpayer is late filing his tax return then the Revenue's time limit remains at nine months from the date of filing the return, whereas the individual's time limit for repairing the return remains at one year after 31 January following the year of assessment.

Example

2.35 Jack files his 1996/97 tax return on 1 June 1998. The due filing date for the return was 31 January 1998. The Revenue may repair the return for a period of nine months, i.e. until 1 March 1999, whereas Jack can only amend the return up to 31 January 1999, i.e. twelve months after the normal filing date.

Notification of an enquiry

2.36 If the Revenue decides to enquire into a return, or into an amendment to the return, then it must give written notice to the taxpayer of its intention. If the return was made by the filing date then the Revenue has twelve months from that date to give notification. If the return was late then the Revenue has twelve months from the quarter date after the date of filing to give notice. The quarter dates are 31 January, 30 April, 31 July, 31 October [*TMA 1970, ss 9A(1), 12AC(1)*].

Example

2.37 Jack above filed his tax return on 1 June 1998. The following quarter date is 31 July 1998. The Revenue has until 31 July 1999 to issue a notice of enquiry.

2.38 Where the taxpayer amends his tax return after the normal filing date, the Revenue has a power of enquiry into that amendment as though the return had been filed on the date of the amendment.

Example

2.39 Jack above, who filed his tax return on 1 June 1998 for 1996/97, amends that return on 12 December 1998. The quarter date following the date of

2.40   Self-Assessment

amendment is 31 January 1999 and the Revenue can therefore issue a notice of enquiry in respect of the amendment at any time up until 31 January 2000.

2.40   Once the Revenue has issued a notice of intention to enquire into a tax return then no amendments of the self-assessment will be possible until the officer has completed his enquiries into the tax return [new *TMA 1970, s 9(5)*].

Power to call for documents

2.41   When the Revenue has given notice of its intention to enquire into a tax return, the officer conducting the enquiry may at the same time, or at any subsequent time, require the taxpayer to produce such documents as are needed by the Revenue [*TMA 1970, s 19A* inserted by *FA 1994, s 187*]. Such a notice must be in writing and must specify a time of not less than 30 days by which the taxpayer must produce the documents. It will be noted from above that the taxpayer is required to keep all such documents that are used to complete his tax return for the period of potential enquiry. The taxpayer may produce photocopies or facsimile copies of documents, unless the notice specifies that original documents must be produced. The Revenue can take copies of documents provided to them.

A taxpayer may appeal within 30 days against the notice requiring production of documents. The Commissioners may confirm the notice if it is reasonable, or set it aside. Where there is an appeal, the time limit for production of the documents is 30 days from the determination by the Commissioners.

Amendments whilst enquiry continues

2.42   Whilst the Revenue is conducting enquiries into a taxpayer's return, the Revenue will have the power to amend a self-assessment if it believes that the tax shown therein is too low. The Revenue may give notice to the taxpayer to amend the return and thereby require the payment of the tax [*TMA 1970, ss 28A, 28B* inserted by *FA 1994, ss 188, 189*].

Conclusion of enquiry

2.43   Similar powers are available to the Revenue on the completion of the enquiry. It will then notify the taxpayer that enquiries are complete and give the Revenue's conclusions [*TMA 1970, s 28A(5)*]. If the officer is of the opinion that the self-assessed tax is too low, then the officer will issue a notice telling the taxpayer what, in the opinion of the Revenue, the self-assessment should have contained. The taxpayer is then given 30 days to amend his assessment, informing the Revenue of the same. This enables the taxpayer to amend the tax liability upwards or downwards in line with the officer's conclusions or to make other amendments that the taxpayer considers appropriate.

The Revenue then has 30 days following the expiry of the taxpayer's 30-day period for amendment in which to amend the return to make good any shortfall the Revenue believes exists. The taxpayer can appeal against such an amendment.

2.44 If a taxpayer believes that the Revenue has no further grounds for enquiry and should complete the same then he can apply to the Commissioners to ask them to direct the Revenue to issue a notice of completion [*TMA 1970, s 28A(6)*]. Such a notice must include the Revenue's conclusions. The Commissioners must give such a direction unless they are satisfied that the Revenue has reasonable grounds for proceeding with the enquiry. Such a hearing will be conducted in the same way as an appeal, with both sides being heard and presenting evidence.

2.45 Similar provisions apply to partnerships. Any amendment to the partnership statement will also be given to each partner so that each individual is required to amend his own tax return within the same 30-day time limit.

Payment of tax

2.46 The new provisions simplify the payment dates for income tax and capital gains tax. In future, capital gains tax will be due on 31 January following the year of assessment. Income tax will be due on 31 January following the year of assessment, but there will be a requirement in most circumstances to make interim payments on account [*TMA 1970, s 59B* inserted by *FA 1994, s 193*].

The interim payments will be based upon the income tax liability of the previous year, net of payments at source, PAYE, tax credits, etc. One half of the previous year's tax liability will be due on 31 January in the fiscal year of assessment, with a further payment of the same amount due on 31 July following the end of the year of assessment [*TMA 1970, s 59A* inserted by *FA 1994, s 192*].

2.47 Small interim payments will not be required. The Revenue will be given power to make regulations setting out de minimis limits. These have not been announced. They may be absolute or as a proportion of total income. An indication of the possible limits is given by the draft tax guide notes which indicate that payments on account will not be required in the following circumstances:

(a) if the tax deducted at source is more than 90% of the total income tax plus Class 4 NIC; or
(b) if the total tax due is less than £500.

These figures are the tax due for the preceding year but are used to form the basis of the interim payment for the current year.

Special rules apply to the calculation of interim payments for the transitional year of 1996/97 (see Chapter 4). Otherwise the new rules apply from that year.

Example

2.48 Georgina submits her tax return for 1996/97 on 30 January 1998. Her taxation liability for that year is:

2.49 Self-Assessment

	£	£
Income tax		9,250
Capital gains tax		3,000
Class 4 NIC		1,200
		13,450
Less deducted at source	1,800	
paid on account	6,400	8,200
Due 31 January 1998		5,250

With her return, she submits a cheque for the above liability together with an interim payment for 1997/98 calculated in the following way (based upon 1996/97 return figures):

	£
Income tax	9,250
Class 4 NIC	1,200
	10,450
Less deducted at source	1,800
Relevant amount	8,650

(*Note:* the liability is NOT recalculated using 1997/98 rates or allowances)

Due 31 January 1998 50% x 8,650	£4,325
31 July 1998 50% x 8,650	£4,325

Her tax return for 1997/98, submitted on 30 November 1998, shows taxation liabilities of:

	£	£
Income tax		10,400
Capital gains tax		NIL
Class 4 NIC		1,250
		11,650
Less deducted at source	1,750	
payments on account	8,650	10,400
Due 31 January 1999		1,250

Her payment will also include an interim payment for 1998/99 of:

	£
Income tax and Class 4 (as above)	11,650
Less deducted at source	1,750
	9,900

50% thereof = £4,950

If the interim payments exceed the liability then repayment will be made by the Revenue on 31 January following the year of assessment. If repayment is not made by 31 January, interest will be added from that date.

2.49 Where a taxpayer believes that the amount due for the current tax year will be less than in the previous tax year, an application may be made at any time before 31 January following the year of assessment for the interim

Self-Assessment 2.50

payments to be reduced. The interim payment may be reduced to nil by a *TMA 1970, s 59A(3)* claim, or reduced to a specified amount by a *TMA 1970, s 59A(4)* claim. The claim must set out the reason for the application to reduce the interim payments. If appropriate, repayment of tax already paid will be made to the taxpayer at that time. However if a taxpayer fraudulently or negligently makes an incorrect statement in connection with such a claim he will be liable to a penalty not exceeding the excess of the correct tax over the actual tax paid on account [*s 59A(6)*].

It is understood that, in practice, the Revenue will accept all reasonable claims under this section without query.

Example

2.50 Georgina ceases trading on 1 December 1998 due to poor profitability. She estimates that after overlap relief she will have no liability to income tax or Class 4 NIC for 1998/99 on trading income. She makes a claim under *TMA 1970, s 59A(3)* on 1 March 1999 indicating that no interim payments are due.

The Revenue will repay the £4,950 paid on 31 January 1999 and no amount will be due on 31 July 1999.

Her tax return for 1998/99, submitted on 20 December 1999, shows taxation liabilities of:

	£
Income tax	4,100
Capital gains	1,800
Class 4 NIC	700
	6,600
Less deducted at source	1,400
Payable 31 January 2000	5,200

If the Revenue believed that her claim had been made fraudulently or negligently then the maximum penalty would be

	£
Income tax	4,100
Class 4 NIC	700
	4,800
Less deducted at source	1,400
Maximum penalty	3,400

The taxpayer can make a claim under *TMA 1970, s 59A(4)* to reduce payments on account by a stated amount. In those circumstances the maximum penalty for negligent claims would be reduced further by the amounts paid on account. It is expected that the Revenue will only take penalties where the amounts involved are material.

2.51   *Self-Assessment*

2.51   When computing tax payments, it must be remembered that it will not be possible to use such statements as 'as returned' in a tax return. To complete a return for an employed person it will be necessary to have sight of forms P60 and P11D or P9D in order to be able to compute the income tax liability. Thus the self-assessment rules will effectively apply to the collection of underpaid Schedule E in many instances.

2.52   Where a taxpayer amends his self-assessment, including circumstances where the Revenue has repaired the tax return, i.e. given notice to the taxpayer to amend his self-assessment, then the revised tax is payable on the normal due date or 30 days after the making of the revised self-assessment. Interest is of course charged from the normal due date. It should be noted that the amendment to a tax return will affect the amount of interim payments required for the following year, as well as amending the tax due for the year of change.

Chapter 3

The Penalty Regime

Enforcement

3.1 In order to control and police a self-assessment system it is necessary to have a comprehensive armoury of penalties available to the Revenue authority. The proposal for income tax self-assessment is no exception. The Revenue will automatically charge interest from the due date of payment. To compensate, a repayment of interest will be paid on overpaid tax from the due date or payment date, whichever is the later.

In addition to interest for late payment, there will be a surcharge if tax is not paid by 28 days from the final due date. This surcharge increases by a further surcharge of 5% of the tax unpaid six months after the normal due date. Such a surcharge is treated as though it is income tax for the purpose of charging interest. However, a surcharge is not taken in addition to a further tax-geared penalty.

For the first time an automatic penalty applies for failure to file an income tax return by the due date. If a return is not filed by 31 January following the end of the fiscal year, or three months after the date of issue if later (providing full notification of liability has been made), then there will be a penalty of £100. If the return has not been filed by six months after the filing date, a further penalty of £100 is imposed. The Commissioners can set aside the flat penalty if there is a reasonable excuse for failure.

If the failure continues after a year, a penalty can be imposed up to the tax liability that would have been shown in the return. On application by the Revenue to the Commissioners, a daily penalty can be imposed.

Similar penalties apply to each partner for failure to file a partnership return.

The new regime makes it essential that accounts and tax returns are filed by the due date, and that tax is paid by the due date. The penalties for failure to meet such deadlines can be high.

Interest

3.2 Interest is charged on late-paid tax and on any surcharges added to the tax [new *TMA 1970, s 86* substituted by *FA 1994, 19 Sch 23*]. Interest is also charged on penalties, from the due date to the payment date [new *TMA 1970, s 103A*].

3.3 The Penalty Regime

Interest is charged at the normal *FA 1989, s 178* rate on income tax and capital gains tax, and on payments on account from the due date until the payment date.

In the case of a cheque, the payment date is the date it is received by the Revenue, providing it is honoured on presentation [*TMA 1970, s 70A* inserted by *FA 1994, 19 Sch 22*].

Amendments to tax returns

3.3 If a tax return is amended, interest applies from the normal final payment date. However, it would appear that an amendment to a tax return will also amend the interim payments due for the following year, which in itself will give rise to an additional interest charge from the normal payment date to the actual date of payment.

Appeals

3.4 If tax is postponed under an appeal then interest is chargeable from the normal payment date to the actual date of payment.

Interest on overdue tax

3.5 Interest is charged from the due date for payment to the actual date for payment. This applies to interim payments on account under *TMA 1970, s 59A* and to the settlement payment of income tax plus capital gains tax under *TMA 1970, s 59B*.

Interest on interim payments where eventual liability exceeds preceding year liability

3.6 If a taxpayer believes that the interim payments to be made are too high then he may make application to reduce those payments under *TMA 1970, s 59A(3)* or *(4)*. Where a claim has been made under *s 59A(3)* to reduce the interim payment to nil, or under *s 59A(4)* to reduce the payment on account, special rules apply to calculate the interest payable.

Interest will be charged on the basis that the amount collectable on account is the lower of:

(a) the original interim payment (50% of preceding year liability);
(b) one half of the final liability (50% of current year liability).

The interest due will then be calculated on the difference between the actual payment and the deemed interim payment due under the above rule [*TMA 1970, s 86(4) – (6)*].

If the estimate proves to be too low, then interest may be payable from the normal payment date for the interim liability to the actual date of payment, which will normally be the date of the final liability payment.

The Penalty Regime 3.8

In normal circumstances, this means that interest will be charged on the difference between the amount paid and the normal interim payment had a claim for reduction not been made, restricted to one half of the eventual final income tax liability.

Example

3.7 Donna has an income tax liability for 1997/98 of £10,000. Accordingly, £5,000 is payable on 31 January 1999 and 31 July 1999 as payments on account of 1998/99.

She is aware that her income for the current year will be reduced because of falling profits and she makes a claim under *TMA 1970, s 59A(4)* to reduce her interim payments to £3,500 on each occasion, which she pays on time.

Her eventual income tax liability for 1998/99 amounts to £8,200, which she settles with a final payment of £1,200 on 30 January 2000.

Interest will be due on late interim payments as follows:

	£
Original interim payment	5,000
One half of collectable liability	
50% x £8,200	4,100

	£
Difference between actual payment	3,500
and lower of the above	4,100
	600

Interest is due on:

	£
Period 1 February 1999 to 31 July 1999	600
1 August 1999 to 30 January 2000	1,200

Example

3.8 Continuing the above example for 1999/2000, Donna has a liability to pay interim payments of £4,100 on 31 January 2000 and on 31 July 2000. She again makes a *TMA 1970, s 59A(4)* claim to reduce her payments on account to £3,900 on each date. However, her eventual liability for the year 1999/2000 amounts to £9,100, which she settles with a final payment on 20 February 2001.

Interest will be due on interim payments as follows:

	£
Original interim payment	4,100
One half of collectable liability	
50% x £9,100	4,550

3.9 *The Penalty Regime*

	£
Difference between actual payment	3,900
and lower of above	4,100
	200

Thus, although the final payment for 1999/2000 will amount to £9,100 - (£3,900 + £3,900) = £1,300, interest will only be charged on late interim payments of £200 from 31 January 2000 and a further £200 from 31 July 2000 giving interest due on:

	£
Period 1 February 2000 to 31 July 2000	200
1 August 2000 to 31 January 2001	400
1 February 2001 to 20 February 2001	1,300

together with interest on the late paid 2000/2001 interim payment

1 February 2001 to 20 February 2001	4,550

Interest remitted where eventual liability is lower than interim payment

3.9 Similar calculations are to be made where interest is charged on interim payments made late where there is an eventual repayment of tax.

If interest has been charged on late interim payments and eventually there is no liability whatsoever for the year, then all interest charged on late interim payments will be remitted [*TMA 1970, s 86(7)*].

If the interim payments exceed the eventual total liability for the year, and one or both of the interim payments have been paid late, then the interim payments are deemed to have been reduced to one half of the eventual total liability. Insofar as any interest charged relates to the excess of interim payment over revised liability, it will be remitted.

Example

3.10 Ann has a liability to pay interim tax for 1997/98 of £2,100 on each occasion. She makes the payments on 31 March 1998, and 28 October 1998 with interest being charged on late payment of:

First instalment	£36
Second instalment	£51

Her liability for that year is self-assessed at £2,800 with repayment made to her of £1,400.

Interest will be remitted on one half of the repayment (£700) restricted to the interim payment due (£2,100) in respect of each interim payment, i.e. she would receive a repayment of £1,400 plus remitted interest on late payment of:

and 700/2,100 x £36 = £12
    700/2,100 x £51 = £17
                     £29

The new rules on interest apply for 1996/97 except in the case of partnerships, where they apply from 1997/98 onwards.

Surcharges

3.11 To prevent the taxpayer using the Inland Revenue as a cheap form of loan finance, *section 59C* is introduced into *TMA 1970* (by *FA 1994, s 194*).

The new surcharge section provides that where tax remains unpaid 28 days from the due date it shall be increased by a surcharge of 5%. Furthermore, when any tax remains unpaid on the day following the expiry of six months from the due date, the surcharge on the tax then outstanding is a further 5%. The surcharge will not be charged as well as a tax-geared penalty.

3.12 The surcharge will be charged by way of notice served by the Revenue on the taxpayer. The taxpayer may appeal against that notice within 30 days [*s 59C(5)(7)*]. The Commissioners may set aside the surcharge if it appears to them that the taxpayer had a reasonable excuse throughout the period of default for not paying the tax. The inability to pay the tax is not in itself a reasonable excuse. Alternatively, the Board of the Inland Revenue may mitigate or remit the surcharge at their discretion [*s 59C(9)–(11)*].

Interest will be charged on any surcharge not paid within 30 days of the date that the *notice* is issued [*s 59C(6)*]. A surcharge is not charged on late-paid interim payments.

In the same way, if a tax return is repaired by the Revenue or amended by the taxpayer, then the due date for payment becomes 30 days after the notice of amendment.

3.13 Similar rules apply where a self-assessment is amended following enquiries by the Revenue. Such enquiries will result in a notice of completion, which must state the Revenue's conclusions as to the amount of tax which should be contained in the taxpayer's self-assessment. The taxpayer then has 30 days in which to amend his return, and a further 30 days after that in which to pay the tax. If the tax remains unpaid 28 days following the end of that latter period, then a surcharge will be applied.

If the taxpayer disagrees with the Revenue, then the Revenue will themselves amend the assessment. The taxpayer will have the right to appeal against the amendment and the revised *TMA 1970, s 55* will enable postponement of the tax at that time.

A worked example of interest and surcharge

3.14 Susan has a final liability for 1996/97, due 31 January 1998, of £2,100. She pays £1,000 on 28 February 1998. On 31 March 1998 the Revenue issues a

3.15 *The Penalty Regime*

notice of surcharge. She pays a further £600 on 31 May 1998. On 2 August 1998 the Revenue issues a further surcharge notice. Susan pays the balance of her liability and surcharges on 31 August 1998.

Her interest and surcharge payable will be (assuming 10% p.a. interest):

	£	£
Surcharge		
On tax outstanding at 28 February 1998		
5% x £1,100	55	
On tax outstanding at 31 July 1998		
5% x £500	25	80
Interest		
1 February to 28 February		
10% x 28/365 x £2,100	16	
1 March to 30 April		
10% x 61/365 x £1,100	18	
1 May to 31 May		
10% x 31/365 x £1,155	10	
(including surcharge unpaid after 30 days)		
1 June to 31 August		
10% x 92/365 x £555	14	58
		138

(Note that the second surcharge is paid within 30 days of the notice and therefore does not attract interest.)

Assessments and determinations

Determination of tax where no return delivered

3.15 Under self-assessment, the Revenue will not normally issue an assessment to the taxpayer. However, if a taxpayer does not file a tax return then the Revenue will be able to raise a determination on him under *TMA 1970, s 28C* [inserted by *FA 1994, s 190*]. Such a determination will be treated as if it were a self-assessment. The Revenue will make the determination to the best of its information and belief and may be based upon income tax or capital gains tax for the year of assessment.

Any tax payable under the determination is deemed to be due on the same day as the normal tax which would have been due had the taxpayer self-assessed. This tax is collectable and cannot be postponed. A self-assessment filed within twelve months of the date of determination will supersede the determination.

The Revenue cannot issue a determination more than five years after the 31 January following the year of assessment.

3.16 The above provisions deal with the situation where the taxpayer has not filed a tax return. It should be remembered that the onus is on the taxpayer to report sources of income within six months from the end of the fiscal year in which those sources arise. Failure to do so will give rise to the penalties set out in *TMA 1970, s 7*, i.e. an amount not exceeding the amount assessable for the year or the amount not paid by the due date (see also 3.21 below).

Assessment where a loss of tax is discovered

3.17 A less common situation may well be where the taxpayer has not notified the Revenue of a source of income and therefore a tax return has not been submitted. This situation is dealt with by the new *TMA 1970, s 29* [as substituted by *FA 1994, s 191*] which provides that the Revenue may raise an assessment where a loss of tax is discovered by them.

As the enquiry system does not of itself give rise to penalties it must be expected that the Revenue will be looking to make 'discoveries' during the course of an enquiry, thus enabling it to issue assessments and charge penalties.

An assessment may be raised if an officer discovers:

(a)   that any profits which ought to have been assessed to tax have not been assessed;
(b)   that an assessment to tax is or has become insufficient; or
(c)   that any relief which has been given is or has become excessive [*s 29(1)*].

It is not a discovery if the taxpayer has delivered a return and that return was made in accordance with the normally accepted accounting practice prevailing at the time when the return was made.

3.18 Furthermore, if a taxpayer has made a tax return, then unless there has been fraudulent or negligent conduct on behalf of the taxpayer or somebody acting on his behalf, the Revenue is precluded from making a discovery after it has informed the taxpayer that it has completed its enquiries into the taxpayer's return. In the same way, if the period in which the Revenue could commence enquiries has expired, the Revenue cannot make a discovery unless it can show fraud or negligence. If an enquiry has been conducted into a taxpayer's return and the Revenue has issued notice that it has completed its enquiries, then the Revenue again is precluded from making a discovery (except for fraud or negligence), unless the discovery could not have been reasonably expected to have been made on the basis of the information available to the Revenue during the course of the enquiry.

For the purpose of the phrase 'information available to the officer', the Revenue is deemed to have such information available to it if:

(a)   it is contained in a person's tax return, or in any accounts, statement or documents accompanying the return;
(b)   it is contained in any claim made by the taxpayer;
(c)   it is contained in any document, account or particulars which are produced to the Revenue for the purpose of the enquiry;
(d)   it has been provided to the Revenue in the above circumstances in either of the two immediately preceding returns; or

(e) it is information notified in writing by the taxpayer to the Revenue during the same period [*s 29(6)(7)*].

If the Revenue make a discovery then penalties will arise under the existing legislation.

Penalty for late filing of tax return

3.19 It must be remembered that the tax return must be filed by 31 January, or three months after the date of issue. This is an absolute time limit and will result in a flat rate penalty of £100 if the filing date is missed. If the failure continues for a further six months the penalty will be increased by a further £100. The fixed penalties cannot exceed the tax liability for the year. If the tax return has not been filed one year after the filing date then the penalty is increased to the tax liability shown by the return. That penalty is appealable to the Commissioners [new *TMA 1970, s 93* substituted by *FA 1994, 19 Sch 25*].

3.20 In addition, the Revenue can apply to the Commissioners for a penalty of up to £60 per day for continued failure to file a tax return, but if this application is made before the second £100 penalty then that second penalty will not be applied.

The Commissioners can on appeal set aside the flat rate penalty if it appears to them that there is a reasonable excuse for the failure to file a tax return during the period of default. Similar penalties also apply to partnership returns [*TMA 1970, s 93A* inserted by *FA 1994, 19 Sch 26*].

Notification of chargeability

3.21 The penalty for failure to notify chargeability by 6 October following the end of the fiscal year in which the income arises is a penalty of an amount up to the tax which remains unpaid as at 31 January following the year of assessment [new *TMA 1970, s 7(8)* substituted by *FA 1994, 19 Sch 1*]. This rule is introduced from 1995/96. It should be noted that in the case of a new business notification will be required before the end of the first trading period in many instances.

Example

3.22 Jenny commenced trading on 1 November 1995. She makes her accounts up to 31 October 1996. The income first arose in the fiscal year 1995/96 and therefore the latest date for notification is 5 October 1996.

If the above example had been one year later under self-assessment then payment for the Schedule D tax liability based upon the period 1 November 1996 to 5 April 1997 would be due on 31 January 1997, a mere three months after the end of the first period of account. It will be seen that if the first trading period had been the year ended 28 February 1998, payment would actually be due on 31 January 1998, before the end of the first accounting period. Obviously the taxpayer would have to use a best estimate and correct that estimate after the end of the period, with a charge to interest on any underpayment.

Keeping of records

3.23 To complement this brief review of penalties, it should be noted that records must be maintained for one year from the 31 January following the fiscal year of assessment, increased if the return is filed late to the anniversary of the quarter date of filing, or in the case of a trade, profession, vocation or letting for five years from 31 January following the year of assessment. The penalty for failure to retain records is an amount of up to £3,000 [*TMA 1970, s 12B(5)*].

Production of documents

3.24 If a taxpayer is under enquiry, then the Revenue may issue a notice requiring the production of documents that are in the taxpayer's power or possession. If the taxpayer fails to produce documents as required by a notice under the new *TMA 1970, s 19A*, then a penalty will be imposed under the new *TMA 1970, s 97AA* [inserted by *FA 1994, 19 Sch 29*]. This will be a penalty of £50, together with a daily penalty for continued failure of an amount not exceeding £30 per day for each day the failure continues after the date on which the penalty of £50 is imposed. If the penalty is imposed by the Commissioners, the maximum amount is £150 per day.

Interest on penalties

3.25 A new section is introduced into *TMA 1970* at *s 103A* imposing interest upon late payment of penalties. It is charged from the date on which the penalty becomes due and payable until payment [*FA 1994, 19 Sch 33*].

Claims

3.26 Many time limits are altered by the introduction of self-assessment. The general rule becomes that a claim must be made by five years from the 31 January following the end of the year of assessment [*TMA 1970, s 43 (1)* as amended by *FA 1994, 19 Sch 14*]. This is approximately nine weeks shorter than the present time limit of six years. This new general rule is introduced for 1996/97, except for existing partnerships when it applies from 1997/98.

The treatment of such claims is dealt with in a new *Schedule 1A* to the *Taxes Management Act 1970* [inserted by *FA 1994, 19 Sch 35*]. This gives the Revenue the power to determine the form in which claims are made and allows for amendment or alterations to such claims.

However, many claims are to be made in the tax return [new *TMA 1970, s 42* substituted by *FA 1994, 19 Sch 13*]. As that return must be complete and final by twelve months after the 31 January following the end of the year of assessment, the normal time limit will become one year and ten months after the end of the fiscal year for many such claims.

Error or mistake claims

3.27 In the past such claims would have been available under an error or mistake claim [*TMA 1970, s 33*]. However it is provided that error or mistake claims are specifically excluded where the claim should have been made in the tax return, and that for other allowable claims the time limit shall be five years from the 31 January following the end of the year of assessment.

Error or mistake claims will not be allowed where a tax return has been completed on the basis of the practice generally prevailing at the time that the tax return was made [*FA 1994, 19 Sch 8*].

3.28 Similar rules apply for partnership statements as well as partnership returns, allowing for errors or mistakes to be corrected within five years of the filing date. The claim is made by the representative partner and if the partnership statement is amended the amendment is binding on all partners and the Revenue will give each partner a notice of the amendment so that they can amend their own self-assessment [*TMA 1970, s 33A* inserted by *FA 1994, 19 Sch 9*].

Assessments for 1995/96 and earlier years

3.29 If an assessment to income tax or capital gains tax for 1995/96 or any earlier year is issued after 6 April 1998, then the interest and surcharge provisions of self-assessment will apply [*TMA 1970, s 59C* and *s 86* as amended by *FA 1995*]. This means that if a tax return was issued and completed for that earlier year by 31 October following the year of assessment (and therefore *TMA 1970, s 88* cannot apply) interest will run under the reused *TMA 1970, s 86* from 31 January following the end of the year of assessment.

Chapter 4

Payments of Tax for 1996/97

Payments on account in 1996/97

4.1 As set out in Chapter 2, the taxpayer is required to make interim payments on account of tax on 31 January in the year of assessment and 31 July following the year of assessment. These amounts are normally based upon the tax assessed for the preceding year, after deduction of tax paid at source by PAYE, etc. A final settling up payment is due on 31 January following the year of assessment. That payment will include the capital gains liability. The Class 4 NIC liability is treated as income tax and forms part of the payment on account.

4.2 The new rules are introduced with effect from 1996/97 for payments on account (for partnerships the new rules apply for 1997/98). However, the first self-assessment will be undertaken with the 1996/97 tax return, which will not be issued until after 5 April 1997. Accordingly, special rules will be needed to deal with payments in the year 1996/97.

As the taxpayer will not have the information to hand for 1995/96, the Revenue intends to calculate the payments on account to be made and to issue payment demands in the normal way.

The payment on account rules set out in *TMA 1970, s 59A* are therefore amended by *FA 1995, 21 Sch*.

Higher rate liability

4.3 One of the effects of the introduction of self-assessment is that a higher rate tax liability on investment income is payable one half on 31 January in the year of assessment and one half on 31 July following the year of assessment, compared with the previous rule of the whole amount payable on 1 December following the year of assessment. Accordingly, for 1995/96, taxpayers will pay their higher rate tax liability on 1 December 1996. The liability for 1996/97 will be payable on 31 January 1998. It must be remembered that the liability for 1997/98, based upon 1996/97, will be payable one half on 31 January 1998 and one half on 31 July 1998. Any additional amount payable or repayable will be due on 31 January 1999.

4.4 *Payments of Tax for 1996/97*

Schedule A and Schedule D Cases III to VI

4.4 A further change occurs with Schedule A and Schedule D Cases III to VI. Normally the tax on that income would have been payable on 1 January in the year of assessment. Under self-assessment, again the amount due becomes payable on 31 January in the year and 31 July following the year of assessment.

Therefore, for the 1995/96 assessment, the Schedule A liability will be due on 1 January 1996, with a correcting assessment issued when the exact liability is known. For 1996/97, the liability will be due on 31 January 1997, based upon the previous year's liability. Any additional amount payable or repayable will be due on 31 January 1998. For 1997/98 the liability will be due one half on 31 January 1998 and one half on 31 July 1998, based on the previous year's liability, with a balancing adjustment on 31 January 1999.

Schedule D Cases I and II

4.5 The payments on account for 1996/97 will be based upon the agreed assessment for the year 1995/96. Note that under self-assessment that liability is not recomputed for changes in rates or allowances in the following year. It would therefore appear that when a practitioner calculates the tax liability for 1995/96, possibly based upon an accounting period such as the year ended 30 April 1994, then the client can be informed that the liability will be due as to:

(a) one half on 1 January 1996 and one half on 1 July 1996 (1995/96 income tax and Class 4 NIC payments); and
(b) one half on 31 January 1997 and a final one half 31 July 1997 (1996/97 income tax and Class 4 NIC interim payments).

The total 1996/97 liability will be calculated on the tax return issued for that year and any adjusting amount will be paid or repaid on 31 January 1998.

Reductions of payment on account

4.6 The taxpayer will be able to make a claim under *TMA 1970, s 59A(3) or (4)* to reduce the amount payable in respect of 1996/97, if he has reasonable grounds for believing that the liability is overstated. The interest and surcharge provisions will apply to late payment in the normal way.

Computation of amount payable in 1996/97

4.7 It is the intention of the legislation to:

(a) provide that an amount will be payable on 31 January 1997 equal to that which would have been payable on 1 January 1996;
(b) provide that an amount will be payable on 31 July 1997 equal to that which would have been payable on 1 July 1996;

(c) provide that the balancing amount of income tax plus the capital gains liability will be payable on 31 January 1998.

Thus, in 1996/97 the higher rate and capital gains tax liabilities are deferred by two months. However, in 1998:

(a) the higher rate assessment for 1996/97 is due on 31 January 1998;
(b) the higher rate assessment for 1997/98 (based upon the 1996/97 figures) is due as to:
 (i) one half on 31 January 1998; and
 (ii) one half on 31 July 1998.

Therefore, for most taxpayers, there will be two higher rate assessments in the same year, payable as to 150% on 31 January 1998 and 50% on 31 July 1998.

Example – Schedule D Case I income only

4.8 John, who is single, has taxable income for 1995/96 of £20,350 based upon the accounts of the year ended 31 May 1994. His income tax liabilities will be payable as follows:

1995/96	£	£	£
Schedule D I		20,350	
Less personal allowance	3,525		
Class 4 NIC	500	4,025	
		16,325	
Income tax			
3,200 @ 20%		640	
13,125 @ 25%		3,281	3,921
Class 4 NIC			
Income	20,350		
Less lower limit	6,640		
At 7.3%	13,710		1,000
			4,921
Payable			
1 January 1996			2,460
1 July 1996			2,461
1996/97			
Interim Payments			
31 January 1997			2,460
31 July 1997			2,461

Assuming that his final assessable income for 1996/97 under transitional rules amounted to £21,940 and that rates of income tax and national insurance were as for 1995/96, John would have the following additional liabilities:

4.9 *Payments of Tax for 1996/97*

	£	£	£
Schedule D I		21,940	
Less personal allowance	3,525		
Class 4 NIC	559	4,084	
		17,856	
Income tax			
3,200 @ 20%		640	
14,656 @ 25%		3,664	4,304
Class 4 NIC			
Income	21,940		
Less lower limit	6,640		
At 7.3%	15,300		1,117
			5,421
Amount due 31 January 1998			
For 1996/97			
Liability for year		5,421	
Paid on account		4,921	500
For 1997/98			
Interim payment			
½ x £5,421			2,710
			3,210
Amount due 31 July 1998			
For 1997/98			
½ x £5,421			2,711

Example with investment income

4.9 Jenny, who is single, has the same income as John, £20,350 for Schedule D Case I in 1995/96, together with the following investment income (assessable):

	1995/96	1996/97
	£	£
National Savings Bank – Schedule D III	4,000	2,900
Dividends (net)	12,800	13,000

Her tax liabilities will be payable as follows:

1995/96		£	
Schedule D I		20,350	
Schedule D III		4,000	
Dividends (gross)		16,000	
		40,350	
Less personal allowance	3,525		
NIC	500	4,025	
		36,325	

Payments of Tax for 1996/97 **4.9**

		Total £	
Income Tax			
3,200 @ 20%		640	
13,125 @ 25%		<u>3,281</u>	
As above		3,921	
4,000 @ 25%		1,000	
<u>3,975</u> @ 20%		795	
24,300			
<u>12,025</u> @ 40%		<u>4,810</u>	
<u>36,325</u>		10,526	
Less tax credits		<u>3,200</u>	
		7,326	

		£	£
Class 4 NIC			
Income	20,350		
Less Lower Limit	6,640		
At 7.3%	<u>13,710</u>		<u>1,000</u>
			<u>8,326</u>

Payable			
1 January 1996			
Sch D I	3,921		
Class 4	<u>1,000</u>		
50% thereof	<u>4,921</u>	2,460	
Sch D III		<u>1,000</u>	3,460
1 July 1996			
Sch D I (as above)			2,461
1 December 1996			
Higher Rate Liability			
12,025 @ 20%			<u>2,405</u>
			<u>8,326</u>
<u>1996/97</u>			
Interim Payments			
31 January 1997			3,460
31 July 1997			<u>2,461</u>
			<u>5,921</u>

Self-assessment			
Schedule D I		21,940	
Schedule D III		2,900	
Dividends		<u>16,250</u>	
		41,090	

4.10 *Payments of Tax for 1996/97*

	£	£
Less Personal Allowance	3,525	
Class 4 NIC	559	4,084
		37,006
Income Tax		
3,200 @ 20%	640	
17,556 @ 25%	4,389	
3,544 @ 20%	709	
24,300		
12,706 @ 40%	5,082	10,820
37,006		
Class 4 NIC		
Income	21,940	
Less lower limit	6,640	
At 7.3%	15,300	1,117
Tax liability		11,937
Less tax credits	3,250	
Paid on account	5,921	9,171
Due 31 January 1998 re 1996/97		2,766
re 1997/98		
Total liability for 1996/97	11,937	
Less tax credits	3,250	
One half thereof	8,687	4,343
Total due 31 January 1998		7,109
Amount due 31 July 1998		
½ x £8,687		4,344

Partnerships

4.10 Assessments for 1996/97 will be issued by the Revenue on an estimated basis. The normal approach and postponement procedures will apply with the first instalment of tax being due on 1 January 1997 and the second instalment on 1 July 1997 payable by the partnership. The partnership will file a partnership statement (see 2.28 above) and return. Each partner will then file a self-assessment tax return before 31 January 1998, paying the balance of any tax due, the tax paid by the partnership being treated as tax deducted at source by the individual partners.

If a partner has other income then payments on account will be required on 31 January and 31 July 1997 in the normal way.

Chapter 5

Current Year Basis of Assessment

Preceding year basis – the reasons for change

5.1 The reforms introduced by the *Finance Act 1994* rank as amongst the most fundamental changes this century in the way in which individuals deal with their tax affairs. When income tax was introduced, the basis of assessment of profits of the self-employed had been the average profits of the three accounts years preceding the year of assessment. This was reviewed on a number of occasions, with a Royal Commission in 1920 recommending the adoption of the preceding year basis of assessment. That commission was attracted to the adoption of a current year basis but concluded that the practical difficulties of assessment and of dealing with the year of change mitigated against its introduction. The commission concluded that the preceding year basis would make the amount of profits assessed correspond more closely to the profits earned and would be 'a very important step in the direction of uniformity and simplicity'. Thus the preceding year (PY) basis of assessment was introduced by Winston Churchill in the *Finance Act 1926*.

5.2 The basis of assessment has been considered many times since the introduction of the preceding year basis. These included the report of the committee on 'The Taxation of Trading Profits' in 1951, which concluded as follows: 'we began our consideration of the problem with a strong predilection for a change to some form of current year basis, and with the help of the board of Inland Revenue we laboured long in an attempt to find a solution. In the end we were driven to the conclusion that, whatever may be the experience of other countries whose size and circumstances differ greatly from those of our own, a current year basis is impractical in this country'.

The 1955 Royal Commission on 'The Taxation of Profits and Income' concluded that unincorporated businesses should remain on a preceding year basis, whereas companies should transfer to a current year basis and accordingly in 1965 corporation tax was introduced on a current year basis. On that change payment remained based upon the previous period between the end of the accounting period and time of payment. This was finally removed by the *Finance Act 1987* which reduced the payment time to a standard nine months for all companies.

5.3 Unincorporated businesses continued to be assessed on the preceding year basis however, with increasing concern about the complexity and inequities of

5.4 Current Year Basis of Assessment

the system. In the case of partnerships, some of the worst excesses of the exploitation of opening and closing year rules were curbed by the introduction by the *Finance Act 1988* of *ICTA 1988, s 61(4)*, ensuring that partnerships that did not elect for continuation basis would be assessed on an actual basis for at least four years following the change of partners.

5.4 Notwithstanding the generous time provisions between the preparation of accounts and eventual assessment (from nine months for a 5 April year end to 20 months for a 30 April year end), many accounts and computations were submitted late to the Inland Revenue. In 1989/90 the Revenue raised approximately three million assessments on the self-employed for that tax year, two million of those assessments using estimated figures. Approximately 600,000 appeals were listed for hearing.

The preceding year basis of assessment is not only costly in terms of compliance and administration but complex in terms of rules. Thus many members of the public are unable to relate their profits as shown in their accounts to their tax assessments. The problem is compounded in the case of partnerships by the concept that the assessment is on the partnership, calculated by reference to the allowances and reliefs of the individual partners, insofar as they are used against partnership income.

If the rules pose difficulties for the professional advisors, they pose equal and rising difficulties for the Revenue. In 1990/91 three and a half million taxpayers had Schedule D I or II income and of that total almost one half did not have professional advice, thus relying upon the staff of the Revenue to compute the assessable profits from the returned income.

Dealing with the Revenue under the old system

5.5 The first Inland Revenue consultative document, 'A Simpler System for Taxing the Self-Employed' in 1991 used the example of Jim Smith a grocer to illustrate how the present system operates.

Jim prepares his financial statements for the year to 31 August and shows profits of £20,000 for the accounting period 1993/94. He also has £400 per month of rental income, and pays gross interest in the tax year 1995/96 on an allowable loan (not principal private residence). Income tax is assumed to be levied at the 25% rate and his personal allowances are assumed to be £4,200. The following table summarises Jim's dealings with the Inland Revenue for his affairs in the tax year 1995/96.

1 September 1995	The Inspector of Taxes makes an assessment for 1995/96. He estimates profits of £25,000 from Jim's grocery business. With the £4,800 of rent, he calculates that the tax due is £6,400.
15 September 1995	Jim decides to appeal against the estimated assessment. He applies to postpone £2,500 of the tax.

Current Year Basis of Assessment 5.7

1 October 1995	The Inspector agrees to the postponement application, leaving Jim with a bill for £3,900.
1 January 1996	Jim pays the first instalment of £2,050.
1 July 1996	Jim pays a second instalment of £1,850.
1 August 1996	The Inspector asks Jim for his return and financial statements for the accounting year ending 31 August 1994.
1 September 1996	The Inspector writes again, warning that Jim's return and financial statements are now overdue.
1 October 1996	Jim is summonsed to appear before the General Commissioners on 1 November 1996.
1 November 1996	The General Commissioners adjourn the hearing of Jim's appeal for one month to allow time for the return and accounts to be produced.
30 November 1996	Jim submits his return for the tax year 1995/96 to the Inspector, accompanied by his financial statements for the accounting year ended 31 August 1994.
1 March 1997	The Inspector finally agrees Jim's figures. He sends Jim a revised assessment for 1995/96 showing income of £24,800. Mortgage interest paid and personal allowances are deducted to arrive at taxable income. The tax due of £4,400 is above the amount Jim paid in instalments earlier. The assessment therefore includes a demand for the balance of tax due of £500 and interest from 1 July 1996.

5.6   The Revenue consultation papers were taken forward with the issue of a second paper in November 1992 described as 'A Simpler System for Assessing Personal Tax'. This paper pursued various ideas to remove the above complexities. After extensive consultation, the Chancellor announced in March 1993 that a current year basis of assessment would be adopted. The *Finance Act 1994* provides the framework to be introduced.

5.7   Any inference in the title of the consultation papers and their objectives that the new system would be simple can easily be dispelled by the 70 pages of legislation, together with the introduction of a second tranche of legislation in the *1995 Finance Act*.

5.8 Current Year Basis of Assessment

Current year basis – the concepts

5.8 The system to be introduced will be known as the 'current year basis'. This is to say, the profits shown by the accounts drawn up in each year will be taken as those for the year to the following 5 April [new *ICTA 1988, s 60* substituted by *FA 1994, s 200*]. Thus, if Jim Smith prepares his accounts for the year to 31 August 1999, these will be treated as the base period for the year 1999/2000.

If accounts are drawn up to 5 April in each year of assessment then actual profits will apply throughout without difficulty or complication. However, if any other accounting date is chosen then special rules will apply for opening years, on change of accounting date, and on cessation.

5.9 Some of the complexities of the new legislation arise from the need to allow complete freedom in the choice of accounting date. There will be freedom to change the accounting date at any time subject to certain anti-avoidance provisions. The government has also taken the opportunity to significantly reduce tax planning opportunities, by introducing a system with the stated objective of taxing precisely the profits earned by a business over the lifetime of the business. This is achieved by calculating the profits that are taxed more than once (to be known as overlap profits) and then by giving a pro-rata credit whenever a change of accounting date results in a period of greater than twelve months being assessed. Any remaining overlap profits will be deducted from the final assessment of the business when it ceases. If inflation is ignored, the result will be that exactly the profits earned by the business will be taxed during the lifetime of the business. As a further simplification, the concept of separate relief for capital allowances is abolished. Under the new provisions, capital allowances will become trading expenses or trading receipts, as for corporation tax.

5.10 The resultant package for the unincorporated business achieves the objectives of allowing complete freedom in choice of accounting date and taxes profits once and once only, but certainly is not simple, and bears very little resemblance to the proposals in the consultation documents.

The new rules

5.11 The new rules apply to all businesses commencing on or after 6 April 1994.

For businesses in existence on 5 April 1994:

(a) 1995/96 will be the last year to which the preceding year basis applies;
(b) 1996/97 will be the transitional year (the assessment will normally be based upon the twelve month average of the profits from the end of the preceding basis period for 1995/96 to the commencement of the current year basis period for 1997/98) (see Chapter 7);
(c) 1997/98 will be the first year in which the assessment will be based upon the accounts ending in the fiscal year (current year basis).

5.12 The new legislation relating to cessations will apply to businesses which commenced on or after 6 April 1994 at all times. The new rules also apply to businesses which commenced before 6 April 1994 and permanently discontinue after 5 April 1999 (see paragraph 6.23 et seq below).

5.13 For businesses which commenced before 6 April 1994 but cease before 6 April 1997, the old rules apply. For those ceasing between 6 April 1997 and 5 April 1999 transitional rules will apply (see paragraph 6.32 et seq below).

5.14 With effect from 6 April 1997, partnerships will no longer be assessed on the profits of the partnership. Each individual partner's share of profits in a period of account will be assessed on him individually.

All partnership expenses and capital allowances will be given against the profits of the partnership. The resultant profits will be allocated by reference to the profit-sharing ratios for the period of account. Where there is a change in the ownership of the partnership and at least one partner carries on the business before and after the change then it will no longer be a cessation for tax purposes. The new rules will apply immediately to partnerships commencing, or deemed to commence, on or after 6 April 1994. Partnerships are discussed in detail in Chapter 10.

5.15 As a result of the move to a current year basis, a number of changes are made to the provisions granting loss relief. Where relief is claimed against other income it will be given against the income of the year of loss or of the preceding year. The loss relief will be taken after capital allowances. The present statutory fiscal year basis of loss relief will be abolished. The new rules will apply from 6 April 1997 for existing businesses and from 6 April 1994 for businesses commencing after that date. For examples and further details of loss relief, see Chapter 11.

5.16 As a result of the introduction of the new rules for Schedule D Case I and II similar provisions are introduced to remove the preceding year basis of assessment from Schedule D Case III, IV and V. These are discussed in detail in Chapter 12.

Dealings with the Revenue under the new system

5.17 To compare the contacts with the Revenue under the new system, Jim Smith, a grocer making his accounts to 31 August 1997, might have the following dealings with the Revenue.

31 January 1998	Jim pays his first interim payment for 1997/98, being 50% of the 1996/97 assessment excluding capital gains tax (he also makes the balancing payment/obtains repayment in respect of 1996/97).
6 April 1998	Jim receives his tax return for the year ended 5 April 1998.

5.18   *Current Year Basis of Assessment*

31 July 1998	Jim makes his second interim payment for 1997/98 (equal to that paid on 31 January 1998).
30 November 1998	Jim submits his tax return for the year 1997/98 to the Inspector of Taxes accompanied by his financial statements for the accounting year ended 31 August 1997 and his computation of self-assessment.
31 January 1999	Jim pays the balancing payment in respect of 1997/98. He also pays 50% of the total liability for 1997/98 excluding capital gains as first interim payment for 1998/99.

Note that if Jim wished the Revenue to assess him, rather than self-assess his liability, then the accounts for the year ended 31 August 1997 and the tax return for the year ended 5 April 1998 must be filed with the Revenue by 30 September 1998.

The above table when compared with the earlier table shows the reduction of involvement of the Revenue in the assessing process. If the self-assessment option is chosen, then the onus of computing the correct liability falls upon the taxpayer or his advisors.

5.18   To make the current year basis of assessment work, it is necessary for accounts to be prepared timeously. In the case of a business making its accounts to the fiscal year end of 5 April there is just under ten months in which to prepare accounts and tax computations together with tax returns. The tax due based upon those figures will then be due as the balancing payment on 31 January following the year with the figures forming the basis of the interim instalments for the coming year. In the case of a business making up its accounts to 30 April the appropriate period of time will be one year and nine months.

Notwithstanding the apparent generous time scale, it must be remembered that where a partnership is involved the accounts must be agreed by the partners together with division of profits in sufficient time to enable the individual partner to complete his personal return and self-assessment. In many instances the use of an early accounting date in the fiscal year, e.g. 30 April will be advisable to give time for proper consideration of all of the issues involved.

Chapter 6

Opening and Closing Years

New principles

6.1 The original proposals in the consultation paper 'A Simpler System for Taxing the Self-Employed' proposed a very rudimentary system whereby there were no adjustments for opening and closing years. Although the proposals had the advantage of simplicity they could have lead to inequity. This would occur where more than one year's income fell into charge in one year of assessment, thus potentially leading to higher rate tax, with another year having nil or limited income and surplus unusable personal allowances.

Overlap relief

6.2 The new legislation abandons the object of simplicity in favour of equality. Consequently, it is necessary to compute the assessments in the first and second years of a new business by reference to special rules. As a result of using computational rules for this period, some profits are assessed more than once. The precise amount of profits assessed more than once are calculated together with the number of days of assessment that overlap. This is known as 'overlap relief' with the profits counted twice known as 'overlap profits' and the number of days involved as the 'overlap period'.

When a business ceases, the overlap profits are treated as a trading expense of the final year of assessment and thereby the actual profits assessed over the life of the business are exactly equal to the actual profits earned by that business. However no account is taken of inflation. Therefore, in times of high inflation the current year basis of assessment will result in a disadvantage to the self-employed, compared with the preceding year basis which in the same circumstances gave an advantage to the self-employed.

Capital allowances and losses

6.3 The new system does however have a number of simplifying features compared with the previous legislation. Capital allowances are treated as a trading expense, with balancing charges treated as trading receipts. All calculations are made on profits or losses adjusted for capital allowances. In the same way the highly complex rules relating to loss relief in opening and closing years are simplified. In the first instance the losses are dealt with after capital allowances (rather than with the option to add capital allowances). Next

6.4 Opening and Closing Years

the previous fiscal year basis of loss relief is abolished and is replaced by a current year basis. Thus there is symmetry between profits and losses for the first time. Finally partnerships are no longer liable to tax on the profits of the partnership but each individual partner is assessed on his own share for the relevant period of account. Accordingly the question of opening and closing years apply to individual partners and the need for continuation elections or otherwise for the partnership is removed.

Apportionments

6.4 *Finance Act 1995, s 121* amends *ICTA 1988, s 72* and provides that where apportionment is necessary such apportionments are to be made on a time basis in proportion to the number of days. Previously such apportionments were made in months or fractions of months.

However if a more accurate measure of profits for any period can be found, e.g. by reference to the transactions which took place during the period, then apportionment by days does not apply [Inland Revenue SAT 1, 1.18 to 1.20].

Use of 31 March as year end

6.5 Where the taxpayer so requests the Revenue is prepared to accept accounts drawn up to 31 March as the equivalent of accounts to 5 April. This will have the effect that

(a)   The profits of the accounts to 31 March each year will be taxed as though they were for the year to the following 5 April.
(b)   For businesses which commence in the period 1 April to 5 April the assessment for year 1 will be nil.
(c)   There will be no overlap profit and no overlap relief for any later year.

[Inland Revenue SAT 1, 1.100]

Opening years

Accounts prepared to 5 April

6.6 To precisely tax the profits of the business over the lifetime of the business without complex opening year rules would have required the compulsory use of 5 April as an accounting date. That date still has much to commend it in terms of simplicity and for many very small businesses and those not using professional advice it will be the only practicable choice. Where accounts are drawn up for the period to 5 April in each year, depreciation is calculated by using the capital allowance rules and adjustments have been made on the face of the accounts for private proportions of expenditure then, providing there are no disallowable items in the account, the profits shown will be the assessable profit for that fiscal year. There are no opening or closing year adjustments, and overlap relief does not apply.

Example

6.7 Alan Brown commenced trading on 1 May 1994, making up his first accounts to 5 April 1995. His profits as adjusted for income tax purposes are:

	£
1.5.94 to 5.4.95	22,000
Year ended 5.4.96	30,000
Year ended 5.4.97	18,000

His assessable profits will be:

		£
1994/95	1.5.94 to 5.4.95	22,000
1995/96	Year ended 5.4.96	30,000
1996/97	Year ended 5.4.97	18,000

Accounts prepared to a date other than 5 April

6.8 Many businesses will not find 5 April to be the most convenient date to which accounts should be drawn up. The new provisions allow any date to be chosen to suit the business needs. However, where a date other than 5 April is used, then in the first fiscal year of the business' life the profits assessed are those earned from the date of commencement to the following 5 April [new *ICTA 1988, s 61(1)* substituted by *FA 1994, s 201*].

6.9 The assessment for the second year will depend upon the accounting date chosen. If the accounts for the first trading period end in the second year of assessment, and the length of that account is less than twelve months, then the basis of assessment for the second year will be the first twelve months of trading [new *ICTA 1988, s 61(2)*].

6.10 In the more normal circumstance of the first period of account being for twelve months or more, with a date ending in the second year of assessment, then the assessment for the second year will be based upon the twelve months ending on the chosen accounting date [new *ICTA 1988, s 60(3)(a)* substituted by *FA 1994, s 200*].

6.11 When a business starts late in one fiscal year, it is quite normal for there to be two fiscal years without any accounting date. In those circumstances the assessment for the second year will be the actual profits of the fiscal year [new *ICTA 1988, s 60(1)*].

For the third and subsequent years of assessment, the basis period will be the accounts ending on the accounting date that falls within the fiscal year [new *ICTA 1988, s 60(2)(3)(b)*].

Short life businesses

6.12 The new rules apply to all businesses commencing on or after 6 April 1994 [*FA 1994, s 218*].

6.13 Opening and Closing Years

If a business commences and finishes in the same fiscal year then the profits will be the amounts earned during the life of the business. If the business has a life of less than two fiscal years, then actual basis applies throughout [new *ICTA 1988, s 63(a)* substituted by *FA 1994, s 204*].

To illustrate the possible variations, it is useful to consider a series of examples.

A business that makes up its accounts to a date twelve months after the date of commencement

Example

6.13 Brenda Clarke commenced trading on 6 May 1994, making up her accounts to 5 May 1995. Her profits as adjusted for income tax purposes are:

	£
Year ended 5.5.95	24,000
Year ended 5.5.96	30,000
Year ended 5.5.97	18,000

Her assessments are:

		£
1994/95	6.5.94 to 5.4.95 335/365 x 24,000	22,027
1995/96	6.5.94 to 5.5.95	24,000
1996/97	Year ended 5.5.96	30,000
1997/98	Year ended 5.5.97	18,000

Overlap profits of £22,027 will carry forward for use on a change of accounting date or cessation, based upon an overlap period of 6 May 1994 to 5 April 1995 (335 days). The only accounts taken into aggregation are of the year ended 5 May 1995. The figures are those adjusted for income tax purposes after the claims for capital allowances.

First accounts ending in fiscal year of commencement

6.14 Many businesses commence trading and make up accounts for a short trading period to the chosen accounting date. Where the first accounting period ends in the fiscal year of commencement then it will be necessary to prepare a second set of accounts before it is possible to compute the first assessment. The assessment for the first trading year is based upon actual profits, and for the second year to the new accounting date, with the overlap profits being calculated on the second accounts.

Example

6.15 Colin Davies commenced trading on 1 June 1994, making up his accounts to 31 December 1994 and annually to that date thereafter.

Opening and Closing Years **6.17**

His adjusted profits are:

	£
7 months to 31.12.94	7,000
Year ended 31.12.95	36,500
Year ended 31.12.96	42,000

His assessable profits will be:

		£
1994/95	1.6.94 to 31.12.94	7,000
	1.1.95 to 5.4.95	
	95/365 x £36,500	9,500
		16,500
1995/96	Year ended 31.12.95	36,500
1996/97	Year ended 31.12.96	42,000

Overlap profits of £9,500 will carry forward, the overlap period being 1 January 1995 to 5 April 1995 = 95 days. Capital allowances will be based upon accounting periods, therefore for the seven months to 31 December 1994 the claim for writing down allowances will be 7/12ths of the annual amount.

First accounts for more than twelve months ending in second year of assessment

6.16 Where accounts are made up for a first period that exceeds twelve months, but ends in the second year of assessment, then the basis period for that second year will be the twelve months ending with the chosen accounting date.

Example

6.17 Freda Gray commenced trading on 1 June 1994 making her accounts up to 30 September each, commencing 30 September 1995.

Her adjusted profits are:

	£
16 months to 30.9.95	24,350
Year ended 30.9.96	16,000

Her assessable profits will be:

		£
1994/95	1.6.94 to 5.4.95	
	309/487 x £24,350	15,450
1995/96	1.10.94 to 30.9.95	
	365/487 x £24,350	18,250
1996/97	1.10.95 to 30.9.96	16,000

6.18 Opening and Closing Years

Overlap profits of £15,450 + £18,250 = £33,700 - £24,350 = £9,350 will carry forward with an overlap period of 1 October 1994 to 5 April 1995 (187 days).

Capital allowances will be based upon accounting periods, therefore for the 16 months to 30 September 1995 the claim for writing down allowances will be 16/12ths of the annual amount.

First accounts ending in the third year of assessment

6.18 If a business chooses an accounting date close to the commencement date, it is often not practicable to prepare accounts for a very short first period. If, for example, a business commences on 1 March and wishes to have a May year end it will not wish to prepare accounts for three months but will be more likely to prepare accounts for 15 months. This may cause problems in calculating the self-assessed profits for the first two years of assessment (see Chapter 2 on self-assessment and Chapter 3 on interest), as it will be necessary to include a best estimate of assessable profits in the tax return so that it may be filed by the due date, and then it will be necessary to 'repair' the return within twelve months. Therefore for a commencement on 1 March 1998 an estimate will be used in the tax return for the year ended 5 April 1998 and tax paid on that estimate on 31 January 1999. The accounts for the period to 31 May 1999 must be submitted to the Revenue by 31 January 2000 to avoid the need for a further estimate for the second year, and to be in time to 'repair' the previous return.

It will be noticed that if accounts are prepared for a first period that ends in the third fiscal year then the filing date can be very short. In the following example only eight months would be available from the end of the accounting period and last day for filing. Interest would be charged from the due date of payment to the actual date. If the estimate is too high then a 'repayment' rate of interest will be used to calculate the interest due to the taxpayer. The calculation of the assessments themselves are straightforward. The first year is based upon the appropriate proportion of profits relating to the actual period falling in the first fiscal year. The second assessment is on the twelve months profits of the first trading period being the fiscal year, and the third year's assessment will be on the twelve months ending on the new accounting date. Capital allowances will be computed for the period of account unless that period exceeds 18 months (see Chapter 8 below).

Example

6.19 Doreen Ely commenced trading on 1 March 1995 making up her first accounts to 31 May 1996 and annually thereafter.

Her adjusted profits are:

	£
15 months to 31.5.96	45,800
Year ended 31.5.97	30,000

Her assessable profits will be:
1994/95
1.3.95 to 5.4.95

	£
36/458 x £45,800	3,600

	£
1995/96	
6.4.95 to 5.4.96	
366/458 x £45,800	36,600
1996/97	
Year ended 31.5.96	
366/458 x £45,800	36,600
1997/98	
Year ended 31.5.97	30,000

Overlap profits of £3,600 + £36,600 + £36,600 = £76,800 - £45,800 = £31,000 will carry forward, based on an overlap period of 1 June 1995 to 5 April 1996 = 310 days. Capital allowances will be based upon the period of account, which being less than 18 months will give a WDA of 15/12ths.

First accounts for less than twelve months ending in second year of assessment

6.20 The timing of the incurring of expenditure is not the only factor that should be considered in opening years. The length of the first accounting period and the number of times in which it falls into aggregation will again affect the assessments and overlap profits. The following example illustrates an instance where there are two overlap profits to be calculated. The second part shows that different assessments can arise on the same adjusted profits. In total the assessments using separate accounts are £824 lower than combining the accounts, but with a corresponding reduction in overlap relief. It must however be remembered that this may not occur in practice, as the capital allowances could be reduced in the second part of the example by virtue of being calculated in two parts. The actual timing of expenditure will determine whether the assessable profits are greater, lesser or the same.

Example

6.21 Eric Fry commences trading on 1 January 1995 making up his accounts to 30 September, commencing 30 September 1995.

His adjusted profits are:

	£
9 months to 30.9.95	2,730
Year ended 30.9.96	23,725
Year ended 30.9.97	30,000

His assessable profits will be:

		£
1994/95	1.1.95 to 5.4.95	
	95/273 x £2,730	950

6.22. *Opening and Closing Years*

		£	£
1995/96	1.1.95 to 31.12.95		
	273 days to 30.09.95 = 2,730		
	92 days to 31.12.95		
	92/366 x 23,725 = 5,963		8,693
1996/97	Year ended 30.9.96		23,725
1997/98	Year ended 30.9.97		30,000

Overlap profits of £950 + £8,693 = £9,643 - £2,730 = £6,913 to carry forward. Overlap periods of 1 January 1995 to 5 April 1995 (95 days) and 1 October 1995 to 31 December 1995 (92 days) = 187 days. Capital allowances will be based on WDA of 9/12ths in the first period.

Note if the first accounts are made up to 30 September 1996 with adjusted profits of £26,455 the assessments will be:

		£
1994/95	1.1.95 to 5.4.95	
	95/639 x £26,455	3,933
1995/96	6.4.95 to 5.4.96	
	366/639 x £26,455	15,152
1996/97	1.10.95 to 30.9.96	
	366/639 x £26,455	15,152

Overlap profits of £3,933 + £15,152 + £15,152 = £34,237 - £26,455 = £7,782. Overlap period of 1 October 1995 to 5 April 1996 (188 days). Revised capital allowances periods of account will be:

  Year ended 31.12.95 WDA 12/12ths
  1.1.96 to 30.9.96   WDA 9/12ths

With the total allowances for the above periods being deducted from the profits of the 21-month period to 30 September 1996.

Where accounts are divided as to nine months followed by a year, a comparison of the resulting assessments with those resulting from the combining of the first two accounting periods is as follows:

	Separate periods	Combined accounts
1994/95	950	3,933
1995/96	8,693	15,152
1996/97	23,725	15,152
overlap profits	(6,913)	(7,782)

6.22 Further factors to consider are the other taxable income and available allowances of the taxpayer. In the above example, if Eric Fry had no other income then he would have unused allowances in 1994/95 if separate accounts were submitted. On the same basis, but with other income, he could well be a higher rate taxpayer in 1996/97. By combining the accounts the profit profile is smoother and therefore allowances are not wasted and higher rate tax is not likely to be incurred.

Commencement of new rules

6.23 For new businesses, the above rules apply to those that commenced trading on or after 6 April 1994. The old rules for the first three years apply to businesses that commenced before that date, even where the second and third years are 1994/95 and 1995/96.

For businesses in existence on 5 April 1994 the new rules apply from 1997/98, with a transitional year of 1996/97 [*FA 1994, s 218*].

6.24   Summary of the opening year rules

YEAR OF ASSESSMENT	BASIS OF ASSESSMENT
Opening Year	Actual (to 5 April)
Second Year	
Accounts ending in year:	
Under twelve months	First twelve months of trading
Twelve months or more	Year ending on accounting date
No accounts ending in 2nd year	Actual (year ended 5 April)
Third year	Year ending on accounting date

Closing years

Overlap relief

6.25 When a period of account is taken into assessment more than once, the profits that are duplicated are eligible for overlap relief. Such an overlap can arise on commencement, on a change of accounting date where the new accounting date is earlier in the fiscal year and under the transitional rules. If there is a change of accounting date such that more than twelve months is taken into account, then overlap relief is deducted from profits on a pro-rata basis (see Chapter 9). Any relief remaining at cessation is taken into account in computing the profits of the final period [*ICTA 1988, s 63A(3)* inserted by *FA 1994, s 205*]. There is no provision for indexation of the overlap relief.

Accounting date of 5 April

6.26 If a business makes up its accounts to 5 April in each year, then there will be no overlap profits and the final assessment will be based on the actual profits from 6 April to the date of cessation [*ICTA 1988, s 63(b)* substituted by *FA 1994, s 204*].

6.27 Opening and Closing Years

Example

6.27 Alan Brown, who makes up his accounts to 5 April each year, ceases to trade on 30 November 2002. His final assessment will be based upon the period 6 April 2002 to 30 November 2002.

Accounting date of other than 5 April

6.28 When a business ceases and the accounting date is not 5 April, the profits to be taken into account for the final year of assessment will be those arising from the end of the basis period ending in the preceding year to the date of cessation [new *ICTA 1988, s 63(b)*]. This period may be more or less than twelve months. Normally, capital allowances will be computed as a balancing charge or a balancing allowance. However, if the final period of account is for more than 18 months, then capital allowances will be claimed for the twelve-month period, with a balancing charge or allowance for the final period.

Example

6.29 Continuing the example of Brenda Clarke at 6.13 above, a business that commenced on 6 May 1994. On commencement overlap profits of £22,027 were calculated. These are now brought forward and relieved against the final assessment. She makes up her accounts to 5 May each year and ceases to trade on 5 May 1998 with final adjusted profits of £26,000 and overlap profits brought forward of £22,027.

	£
Adjusted profits year ended 5.5.98	26,000
Less overlap profits	22,027
Assessment – 1998/99	3,973

Note that if the final profits had been £6,000 the assessment would be:

	£
1998/99	6,000
Less overlap profits	22,027
	NIL
Loss relief available on	16,027

Relief for the loss may be given by way of normal loss relief or terminal loss relief (see Chapter 11).

More than one accounting date in year of cessation

6.30 If the final period of trading is a short period and ends in the same fiscal year as the normal accounting date, then the normal accounting date is ignored and the assessment is based upon the period of the full twelve months from the normal accounting date in the preceding year plus the final period of account, less the overlap profits [new *ICTA 1988, s 60(5)* substituted by *FA 1994, s 200*]. The profits are of course adjusted for capital allowances.

Opening and Closing Years **6.31**

Example

6.31 Take the results of Brenda Clarke shown above and assume that she continued to trade for a further six months, ceasing to trade on 5 November 1998 with adjusted profits of:

Year ended 5.5.98	£26,000
6 months to 5.11.98	£15,000

Then the assessment will be based upon the period from the accounting date ending in preceding year to the date of cessation:

	£
1998/99	
6.5.97 to 5.11.98	
(26,000 + 15,000)	41,000
Less overlap profits	22,027
	18,973

In computing the above figures, capital allowances would be deducted for the year ended 5 May 1998 and a balancing allowance (or charge) deducted or added for the final period. Exactly the same assessments would occur if the accounts had been aggregated.

Example

	Profits	CAs	Adjusted profits
Year ended 5.5.98	36,000	10,000	26,000
6.5.98 to 5.11.98	16,000	1,000	15,000
	52,000	11,000	41,000

based upon a capital allowance computation of:

	Pool £
Brought forward at 6.5.97	40,000
WDA Year ended 5.5.98	10,000
	30,000
Sale	29,000
Balancing allowance	1,000

If one set of accounts had been prepared for the 18 months, the adjusted profits before capital allowances would be £52,000, with a capital allowance computation of:

	Pool £
Brought forward at 6.5.97	40,000
Sale	29,000
Balancing allowance	11,000

and adjusted profits after allowances of £52,000 - £11,000 = £41,000 as above.

6.32 Opening and Closing Years

No accounting date in penultimate year of assessment

6.32 A very common situation will be the closure of a business where accounts are prepared for a final trading period that exceeds twelve months. As a result, there will be no accounts ending in the preceding year. This position is dealt with by *ICTA 1988, s 60(3)(b)*, which provides that the basis period for the year of assessment is to be the period of twelve months beginning immediately after the end of the basis of period for the preceding year. The rule in *ICTA 1988, s 63(b)* then applies, so that the basis period for the year of cessation is the period commencing immediately after the preceding basis period, i.e. that for the penultimate year, to the date of cessation. The overlap profit relief brought forward is deducted from the final assessment, i.e. that for the year of cessation only [new *ICTA 1988, s 63A(3)*].

By comparison, capital allowances are deducted from the period of account as though a trading expense [new *CAA 1990, s 140(2)* substituted by *FA 1994, s 211*]. If the period of account is for more than 18 months then the period of account is divided, for capital allowance purposes only, into a period of twelve months followed by the balance period. The capital allowances computed for those periods are then aggregated and deducted from the adjusted profits before capital allowances for the whole period.

Example

6.33 Susan Taylor, who has made up her accounts to 31 December each year for many years, and who has overlap profits for the period 1 January 1997 to 5 April 1997 of £6,500, ceases to trade on 31 July 1999, with adjusted profits before capital allowances for the 19-month period of £28,300.

On 1 January 1998 she had a pool residue of £16,000. On 30 November 1998 she purchased a computer for £3,200 and on cessation all pool assets were sold for £11,800.

Her capital allowance claims would be:

	Pool £
Forward at 1.1.98	16,000
Additions Year ended 31.12.98	3,200
	19,200
Writing down allowance	4,800
	14,400
Sale Period ended 31.7.99	11,800
Balancing allowance	2,600

Adjusted profits before capital allowances:

19 months to 31.7.99		28,300
Less CAs – Year ended 31.12.98	4,800	
Period ended 31.7.99	2,600	
		7,400
Profits of period of account		20,900

Assessments:

1998/99	Year ended 31.12.98		
	365/577 x £20,900		13,221
1999/2000	1.1.99 to 31.7.99		
	212/577 x £20,900	7,679	
	Less overlap profits	6,500	1,179

The effect of the rules is that any restrictions in the writing down allowance in the penultimate period will merely be reflected in the balancing adjustment and therefore, in most instances, it will be possible to take the pool brought forward and deduct the eventual sale proceeds. It will, of course, be necessary to go through the full calculation if, for example, differing private usage occurs in the relevant periods.

It is not possible to increase (or decrease) the assessment of the final period to take into account overlap relief and the need to have sufficient income to cover personal allowances by revision of the capital allowances. In this instance, simplification reduces the ability of the tax advisor to maximise the use of allowances, or minimise the effect of higher rates of taxation in one period against the other.

Existing businesses ceasing

6.34 If a business was trading on 6 April 1994 and ceases to trade before 6 April 1997, then the normal cessation rules under the old provisions apply [*FA 1994, 20 Sch 3(1)*].

6.35 If such a business continues to trade beyond 6 April 1997, then new rules apply but with special provisions, enabling the Revenue to amend assessments where cessation occurs in the fiscal year 1997/98 or 1998/99 [*FA 1994, 20 Sch 3 (2) (3)*].

Under the transitional rules, if such a business ceases to trade in the fiscal year 1997/98 the normal transitional rules apply for 1996/97 (see Chapter 7 below) and the normal assessment for 1997/98 will be the profits from the accounting date ending in 1996/97 to the date of cessation in 1997/98 [*ICTA 1988, s 63(b)*]. Transitional rules will enable the Revenue to elect that the new rules are disapplied [*FA 1994, 20 Sch 3(2)*]. If the Revenue take this option then the old rules are deemed to apply for 1995/96 and 1996/97, that is to say the assessment will be based originally on the preceding year basis with the Revenue having the option to increase both the penultimate and prepenultimate assessments to actual. The assessment for 1997/98 will then be on the actual basis as under the old rules. It would appear that the Revenue would only apply these provisions when profits are rising and therefore it will normally mean that the actual basis will apply for the 1995/96, 1996/97 and 1997/98 assessments.

6.36 If a business that had commenced before 6 April 1994 ceases in the fiscal year 1998/99 then the new rules with transitional relief apply. However the Revenue will have the option to elect for the 1996/97 assessment to be based upon the actual profits of the year ending 5 April 1997, rather than the

6.37 *Opening and Closing Years*

assessable amount computed under transitional relief. Overlap profit relief will then be granted against the final assessment [*FA 1994, 20 Sch 3(3)*].

Example of cessation after 6 April 1999

6.37 Laura Moore has been in business for many years, making up accounts to 30 June. She ceases to trade on 30 June 2000. Her adjusted profits are:

	Before CAs £	Capital Allowances £	After CAs £
Year ended 30.6.94	10,000	500	9,500
Year ended 30.6.95	14,000 ⎫	600	—
Year ended 30.6.96	16,500 ⎭		—
Year ended 30.6.97	19,000	750	18,250
Year ended 30.6.98			24,000
Year ended 30.6.99			30,000
Year ended 30.6.00			14,200

Overlap profits will be calculated as being 279/365 x £19,000 = £14,524.

Her assessments will therefore be:

			£	£	£
1995/96				10,000 - 500 =	9,500
1996/97	365/731 x (£14,000 + £16,500)			15,229 - 600 =	14,629
1997/98				18,250	18,250
1998/99				24,000	24,000
1999/00				30,000	30,000
2000/01	Year ended 30.6.2000		14,200		
	Less overlap profits		14,524		NIL
	(Loss Relief £324)				

The capital allowance basis periods will be:

| 1995/96 | 1.7.93 to 30.6.94 |
| 1996/97 | 1.7.94 to 30.6.96 |

The capital allowances for 1997/98 will be based on the period of account from 1 July 1996 to 30 June 1997 and are deducted as trading expenes, as are the allowances for all subsequent periods.

In the above example the business ceased after 5 April 1999 and therefore the new rules apply.

Opening and Closing Years **6.39**

Example of cessation in 1998/99

6.38 By comparison, if Laura Moore had ceased on 30 June 1998, with final profits of £24,000, her assessments would have been:

	£	£	£	CAs
1995/96				10,000 - 500
1996/97 transitional profits as above		15,229		
Revenue option to revise to actual				
86/365 x £16,500	3,887			
279/365 x £19,000	14,524	18,411		
Revenue have option for higher assessment			18,411	- 600
1997/98 Year ended 30 June 1997			18,250	
1998/99 Year ended 30 June 1998	24,00			
Less overlap profits	14,524		9,476	

Initially, the 1996/97 assessment will be based upon the transitional profits of £15,229. The Revenue will have the option to increase the assessment to actual. It would appear that interest will run on the tax due on the increased assessment of £3,182 from the normal payment date of 31 January 1998 to the actual date of payment.

The capital allowance basis periods will be:

| 1995/96 | 1.7.93 to 30.6.94 |
| 1996/97 | 1.7.94 to 30.6.96 |

For 1997/98 and subsequent periods, the allowances are deducted as trading expenses of the relevant period.

Her assessments will therefore be:

		£
1995/96	10,000 - 500 =	9,500
1996/97	18,411 - 600 =	17,811
1997/98		18,250
1998/99 (net of overlap relief)		9,476

Example of cessation in 1997/98

6.39 Assume that Laura Moore ceased trading on 30 June 1997, with adjusted profits for the year ended 30 June 1997 of £18,250.

Her assessments would then be:

6.39 *Opening and Closing Years*

		Without Election	With Revenue Election Actual	Original
	£	£	£	£
1997/98	18,250			
Less overlap profits	14,524	3,726		
Actual				
86/365 x £18,250			4,300	
1996/97		15,229		
Actual (as above)			18,411	14,000
1995/96		10,000		10,000
Actual				
280/366 x £16,500 =	12,622			
86/365 x £14,000 =	3,298		15,920	

As the assessable profits under the old provisions are higher than under the new provisions, the Revenue will elect for the old rules to apply. The resulting assessments will therefore be:

1995/96	£15,920	-	£500	=	£15,420
1996/97	£18,411	-	£600	=	£17,811
1997/98					£4,300

Self-assessment rules do not apply to 1995/96 and therefore it would not appear that there will be any interest charge on the additional assessment of £5,920 for that year providing the assessment is issued by 6 April 1998; otherwise interest runs from 31 January 1997. However self-assessment rules will apply to the year 1996/97. The transitional provisions in *Schedule 20* only disapply the current year rules and therefore interest will be charged on the additional tax based upon £3,182 for the year 1996/97 from 31 January 1998. It is therefore essential that accounts are filed timeously in such circumstances to minimise the effects of interest.

In the above example it has been assumed that the quantum of capital allowances remain constant even though the basis periods change. For example with cessation on 30 June 1997 the basis periods would become

| 1995/96 | 1.7.93 | to | 5.4.96 |
| 1996/97 | 6.4.96 | to | 5.4.97 |

after an election for the actual 'old' basis by the Revenue. Without that election the basis periods would have been

| 1995/96 | 1.7.93 | to | 30.6.94 |
| 1996/97 | 1.7.94 | to | 30.6.96 |

The 1997/98 capital allowances would be based on the balancing adjustment on cessation and deducted from the profits to arrive at the adjusted profits for taxation.

Chapter 7

Transitional Rules for Existing Businesses

Existing businesses

7.1 Businesses already trading on 5 April 1994 will be on a preceding year basis until the fiscal year 1995/96. To move to the current year basis of assessment, the year 1996/97 will be a transitional year. The year 1997/98 will be the first year of assessment to which the current year basis fully applies.

The fiscal year 1996/97

7.2 The Revenue has clearly given much thought to the problem of the transitional year. The basic simple concept is that the preceding year basis period and the current year basis period for the year 1996/97 should be aggregated, with 50% of the profits being assessable [*FA 1994, 20 Sch 2*].

Overlap relief on transition

7.3 However, if a business had used the preceding year basis closing year rules and had an accounting date other than 5 April then more than twelve months of accounts would have dropped out of assessment. For example, a business making up its accounts to 30 April in each year and having an initial accounting period of twelve months would have had assessments of:

Year 1 – 1 May to 5 April following
Year 2 – Year ended 30 April
Year 3 – Year ended 30 April

Thus, the first set of accounts would effectively have been assessed for two years eleven months giving an overlap of 23 months. The simple transitional rules would give a reduction of that period of twelve months but would not give credit for the remaining overlapped opening assessments.

7.4 To give relief for this additional period, the new provisions relating to overlap profits and periods are brought into play. Insofar as the assessable profits for the year 1997/98 relate to a period falling before 6 April 1997, then the profit for that earlier period will be the overlap profit, before deduction of capital allowances, and the number of days before 6 April 1997 will be the overlap period [*FA 1994, 20 Sch 2(4) (4A)* as amended by *Finance Act 1995*].

7.5 Transitional Rules for Existing Businesses

Example of transitional year without change of accounting date

7.5   Laura Moore has been in business for many years, making up her accounts to 30 June in each year.

		Capital Allowances	
Her adjusted profits are:	Before CAs		After CAs
	£	£	£
Year ended 30.6.94	10,000	500	9,500
Year ended 30.6.95	14,000 ⎫	600	
Year ended 30.6.96	16,500 ⎭		
Year ended 30.6.97	19,000	750	18,250

Her assessments will be:

£			
1995/96	10,000 - £500	=	£9,500
1996/97			
365/731 x (14,000 + 16,500)	15,229 - £600	=	£14,629
1997/98	18,250		

Overlap profits will be:

   279/365 x 19,000 = £14,524

based upon an overlap period of 1 July 1996 to 5 April 1997 = 279 days.

The capital allowance basis periods will be:

   1995/96 1.7.93 to 30.6.94
   1996/97 1.7.94 to 30.6.96

The capital allowances for 1997/98 will be based on the period of account 1 July 1996 to 30 June 1997.

Although additions and disposals are taken into the 1996/97 basis period for the two years ended 30 June 1996, only one year's allowances will be available under the old provisions. The technical basis period will be the period 1 July 1995 to 30 June 1996 together with a gap period. Such a gap period is then added to the later basis period [CAA 1990, s 160(3)(b) old provisions]. For 1997/98 the profits will be those after capital allowances, with the allowances for the year ended 30 June 1997 being treated as trading expenses.

Change of accounting date in the transitional period

7.6   To enable businesses to use the simpler fiscal year basis, it will be permissible to change the accounting date during the transitional period. The number of days between the last day of the preceding year basis period for the fiscal year 1995/96 to the new accounting date will be calculated. The profits then assessable for 1996/97 will be:

Transitional Rules for Existing Businesses 7.8

$$\text{Aggregate profits for the period} \times \frac{365}{\text{Total number of days in the period}}$$

Because the new rules for capital allowances do not come into force until 1997/98, the profits will be taken for all of the above periods before deducting capital allowances. The long basis period in the transitional year will only give rise to one year's writing down allowances.

Example of transitional year with change of accounting date

7.7 If preferred, it will be possible to prepare accounts to 5 April 1997 (or any other date). In those circumstances the period of time between the end of the basis period for 1995/96 and 5 April 1997 (or chosen date) will be averaged, with 365 days of that period being used as the basis of assessment.

Example

7.8 Maurice Norton has been in business for many years, making up accounts to 30 June. He will change his accounting date to 5 April.

His adjusted profits are:

	£
Before Capital Allowances:	
Year ended 30.6.94	10,000
Year ended 30.6.95	14,000
Year ended 30.6.96	16,500
Period ended 5.4.97	13,950
After Capital Allowances:	
Year ended 5.4.98	18,250

His assessments will be:

	£
1995/96	10,000
1996/97	
365/1010 x (14,000 + 16,500 + 13,950)	16,063
1997/98	18,250

There will be no overlap profits or overlap period.

The capital allowance basis periods will be:

1995/96	1.7.93 to 30.6.94
1996/97	1.7.94 to 5.4.97

The capital allowances for 1997/98 will be based on the period of account 6 April 1997 to 5 April 1998.

7.9 Transitional Rules for Existing Businesses

In this instance the additions and disposals of the period 1 July 1994 to 5 April 1997 will be taken into the capital allowance computation for 1996/97. Again note that the profits for the year ended 5 April 1998 will be net of capital allowances. Technically there is no reference to a base period for 1997/98 but to the period of accounts of the year ended 5 April 1998.

Anti-avoidance

7.9 The anti-avoidance provisions will apply when profits are artificially moved from the period before averaging into the transitional averaging period, or if profits are moved backwards into a period of account that forms the basis of the transitional overlap relief.

The Inland Revenue will be looking to apply the anti-avoidance legislation in the following circumstances:

(a) any change or modification of an existing accounting policy (e.g. a change in the basis of valuation of trading stock) but excluding any change of accounting date which brings the end of the basis period for 1996/97 closer to 5 April 1997 [FA 1995, 22 Sch 14(2)];
(b) any change of business practice i.e. any change in an established practice of a trade as to:
  (i) the obtaining of goods or services;
  (ii) the incurring of business expenses;
  (iii) the supply of goods or services;
  (iv) the invoicing of customers or clients;
  (v) the collection of debts;
  (vi) the obtaining or making of payments in advance or payments on account [FA 1995, 22 Sch 14(3)];
(c) any self-cancelling transaction including an agreement for the sale or transfer of trading stock or working progress or the acquisitional grant of an option which is subsequently exercised to buy back or re-acquire trading stock or work in progress [FA 1995, 22 Sch 15 and 16];
(d) any transaction with a connected person [FA 1995, 22 Sch 15].

The anti-avoidance provisions do not apply where:

(a) the transaction is entered into solely for bona fide commercial reasons. The obtaining of a tax advantage is specifically stated not to be a bona fide commercial reason;
(b) the main benefit from the transaction that could reasonably be expected was not a tax advantage;
(c) the profits moved fall within the de minimis exemptions to be announced in 1997 [FA 1995, s 22 Sch].

If profits are artificially moved into the transitional period then the 1996/97 assessment will be calculated in the normal manner. The assessment will then be increased by 1.25 x the complementary percentage of the profits identified as being moved. The complementary percentage is [1 - 365/the number of days in the transitional period)] expressed as a percentage. The effect of the above is to impose an automatic penalty equal to 25% of the tax saving that the taxpayer sought to achieve by shifting profits.

In the same way, if profits are moved into the transitional overlap period, the 1997/98 assessment will be based upon the profits as returned by the taxpayer but the overlap profit relief will be reduced by 1.25 x the increase in the overlap profit resulting from profits having been moved into that base period. Again there is an automatic 25% penalty.

In addition to the above anti-avoidance rules the provisions also apply to movements of income under Schedule D Case III to V and to interest paid by individual partners on the refinancing of partnership borrowing.

The purpose of the anti-avoidance legislation penalty is to ensure that taxpayers do not gamble on making such transactions on the assumption that they cannot be worse off. If the anti-avoidance provisions are triggered there will be an automatic increase in the amount payable.

Should you change your accounting date to 5 April?

7.10 The transitional relief interacts with the overlap relief for closing years and therefore two computations are necessary to precisely determine which accounting date will be most advantageous.

The first calculation requires the comparison of the average rate of earnings in the transitional period with the average rate of earnings for the period of account ending in the fiscal year 1997/98.

If the average rate of profit is rising then it will be advantageous to retain the existing accounting date.

If the average rate of profit is static or falling then it will be advantageous to make accounts to 5 April 1997.

However, the above calculation also affects the overlap relief in the year of cessation. Transitional rules will apply for cessations that occur during 1997/98 and 1998/99. For businesses that cease before 6 April 1998, the Revenue may disapply the new rules and effectively assess 1995/96, 1996/97 and 1997/98 on an actual basis. For businesses that cease in the fiscal year 1998/99, the new rules will apply with computation of overlap profits for which relief is given in 1998/99. The Revenue, however, will exercise their option to assess the actual profits in the year 1996/97 if they are higher than the transitional profits. For examples of these provisions, see 6.37 et seq above.

7.11 The second calculation to determine the accounting date for the transitional period requires the comparison of the average rate of profits during the period of account for 1997/98 with the average rate of profits at cessation. Clearly, if a business is not likely to cease within the next five years (and after 5 April 1999) then this calculation will not be practicable and should be ignored. The conclusion from this test would be:

7.12 Transitional Rules for Existing Businesses

If the average rate of profits at cessation is higher than in the period of account ending in 1997/98, the adoption of accounts to 5 April 1997 will be advantageous.

If the average rate of profits at cessation is the same or lower than the average rate for the period of account 1997/98, no change should be made to the existing accounting date.

Example of rising profits

7.12 To illustrate the above with figures, using the example of Laura Moore above, the first test will show:

Laura Moore has a daily rate of earnings during the transitional period of:

$$\frac{£30,500}{731} = £41.72$$

Her daily rate of earnings during the period of account forming the basis of 1997/98 is:

$$\frac{£18,250}{365} = £50.00$$

This means that her assessment will be lower by keeping the existing accounting date, which, as shown above, gave assessments of:

	£
1996/97	15,229
1997/98	18,250
With overlap profit relief carried forward of	14,524

By comparison, say Laura Moore decided to change her accounting date to 5 April and achieved the following adjusted profits:

	£
Year ended 30.6.95	14,000
Year ended 30.6.96	16,500
Period ended 5.4.97	14,524
Year ended 5.4.98*	22,645

(*86/365 x £18,250 = £4,300 + 279/365 x £24,000 = £18,345)

Her assessments would be:

	£
1996/97 (14,000 + 16,500 + 14,524) x 365/1010 =	16,271
1997/98	22,645

If the accounting date adopted was 5 April, then there would be no possibility of the actual profits for the final period from 1 July to 5 April preceding the year of cessation exceeding the overlap relief brought forward of £14,524.

Transitional Rules for Existing Businesses 7.14

The effect of the change has been to increase the assessment for 1996/97 by £1,024 (i.e. £16,271 (revised assessment) compared with £15,229 (original assessment)) and for the year 1997/98 by £4,395 (i.e. £22,645 compared with £18,250). In most instances taxpayers will prefer to have the lower assessments now rather than gamble on potential savings at an unknown date in the future.

Example of declining profits

7.13 If Laura Moore's profits had been declining the reverse would apply. For example if her adjusted profits had been:

	£
Year ended 30.6.95	14,000
Year ended 30.6.96	16,500
Year ended 30.6.97	9,125

Then the average rates of earnings during the transitional year with the normal accounting date would be £41.72 as above, but with average earnings in the 1997/98 base period of:

$$\frac{£9,125}{365} = £25$$

It would then be necessary to go on to check the position with a change of accounting date. If the profits were:

	£
Year ended 30.6.95	14,000
Year ended 30.6.96	16,500
Period ended 5.4.97	6,975
Year ended 5.4.98	8,600

then the transitional assessments would be:

1996/97 (14,000 + 16,500 + 6,975) x 365/1010	13,543
1997/98 Year ended 5.4.98	8,600 with no overlap profits

Comparison with the unchanged accounting date gives a reduction for the 1996/97 assessment from £15,229 to £13,543 = £1,686.

In this instance, there is also a reduction in the 1997/98 assessment from £9,125 down to £8,600, a saving of £525.

Businesses not on PY basis for 1995/96

7.14 If a business is on an actual basis for 1995/96, then the basis period for 1996/97 will be actual, that is with a current year basis applying for 1997/98.

7.15 Transitional Rules for Existing Businesses

This could occur because of a partnership change without a continuation basis election. This is illustrated in Chapter 10 at 10.19 below. The same provision would apply to a new business that commenced before 6 April 1994 and which elected for an actual basis to apply to the second and third years of assessment under *ICTA 1988, s 62*.

Example

7.15 Maurice Jones commenced his trade on 1 May 1993, making up his accounts to 30 April each year. He has elected for actual basis to apply for 1994/95 and 1995/96.

His adjusted profits before capital allowances are:

	£
Year ended 30.4.94	27,375
Year ended 30.4.95	21,900
Year ended 30.4.96	15,372
Year ended 30.4.97	22,265

His capital allowances are:

Year of Assessment	Basis Period	£
1993/94	1.5.93 to 5.4.94	950
1994/95	6.4.94 to 5.4.95	1,310
1995/96	6.4.95 to 5.4.96	1,420
1996/97	6.4.96 to 5.4.97	1,200

For 1997/98 the period of account will be the year ended 30 April 1997, thus giving an entitlement to one full year's writing down allowances, but additions and disposals will only be included for the period 6 April 1997 to 30 April 1997. His capital allowances deductible from profits for that period are £1,095.

His assessments will be:

			£	£
1993/94	1 May 1993 to 5 April 1994			
	Schedule D I 340/365 x £27,375		25,500	
	Less capital allowances		950	24,550
1994/95	6 April 1994 to 5 April 1995			
	Schedule D I			
	25/365 x £27,375	1,875		
	340/365 x £21,900	20,400	22,275	
	Less capital allowances		1,310	20,965
1995/96	6 April 1995 to 5 April 1996			
	Schedule D I			
	25/365 x £21,900	1,500		
	341/366 x £15,372	14,322	15,822	
	Less capital allowances		1,420	14,402

Transitional Rules for Existing Businesses 7.15

		£	£
1996/97	6 April 1996 to 5 April 1997		
	Schedule D I		
	25/366 x £15,372 1,050		
	340/365 x £22,265 <u>20,740</u>	21,790	
	Less capital allowances	<u>1,200</u>	20,590
1997/98	Year ended 30 April 1997		
	Profits before capital allowances	22,265	
	Less capital allowances	<u>1,095</u>	21,170

Overlap relief is available for 340 days, i.e. for the period 1 May 1996 to 5 April 1997, being 340/365 x £22,265 = <u>£20,740</u>.

Chapter 8

Capital Allowances

The changes

8.1 To facilitate the introduction of self-assessment, the principle of having a separate regime for the calculation of depreciation on fixed assets is simplified. Much of the complexity of the existing capital allowance legislation arises from the need to ensure that there is no duplication of additions or disposals of assets, nor gap periods in which such items could fall out of account. With the move to assessments that exactly equal the actual profits earned by the business over the life of the business, the potential for manipulation is reduced and therefore it is possible to introduce a system whereby capital allowances will be treated as trading expenses and balancing charges as trading receipts. This is done by rewriting *section 140* of the *Capital Allowances Act 1990*. Allowances for individuals and partnerships will therefore be given in a broadly similar way to the granting of allowances for corporation tax purposes.

Deduction as a trading expense

8.2 As a result of these changes, capital allowances will no longer be dealt with separately but instead will be deducted in arriving at the adjusted profits, and the adjusted profits will be taken into account for all calculations from the introduction of the new system [new *CAA 1990, s 140(2)* substituted by *FA 1994, s 211*]. The only exception is that transitional overlap relief is calculated on profits before capital allowances [*FA 1995, s 122(3)*].

Period of account

8.3 The previous concept of basis period for capital allowances is abolished and instead the chargeable period will be the period for which the accounts are drawn up [new *CAA 1990, s 160* substituted by *FA 1994, s 212*].

Because capital allowances are based upon a period of account, the writing down allowance will be given by reference to the length of the period of account [*FA 1994, s 213*]. Thus, if accounts are made up for a nine-month period, 9/12ths of writing down allowances will be granted. In the same way, if a period of account is made up for 16 months, allowances will be calculated as 16/12ths of writing down allowance. To prevent manipulation to achieve higher allowances, it is provided that a period of account for capital allowance purposes cannot exceed 18 months [new *CAA 1990, s 160(4)*]. If the period of

Capital Allowances 8.7

account does exceed 18 months then for the purpose of calculating capital allowances it is divided into periods of twelve months, with the balance period having restricted writing down allowances. As the adjusted profits for the period of account is used after capital allowances, it would appear that all of the capital allowances so calculated are deducted from the adjusted profits to arrive at the figure to be brought into the assessment computation.

Claims for capital allowances

8.4 Claims for capital allowances will be made in the tax return [new *CAA 1990, s 140(3)*]. Under self-assessment, this means that capital allowance claims will usually have to be finalised by twelve months after the normal filing date for the tax return, i.e. twelve months after 31 January following the end of the fiscal year of assessment. However, in respect of certain claims, e.g. an election to treat plant as a short-life asset, there is an overriding two-year time limit which applies from the end of the period of account. Therefore, for practical purposes, the time limit should be considered to be the earlier of two years from the end of the period of account and the date above.

Notification of expenditure

8.5 It should be noted that following the *Finance Act 1994*, if notification of the incurring of expenditure is not made to the Inspector within the relevant time limit, then the expenditure will not give rise to allowances in the period in which it was incurred, but instead will be deemed to be purchased in the period of account for which a valid notice of acquisition has been given, providing the asset is still owned in the later period [*FA 1994, s 118*].

Introduction of new rules

8.6 The new provisions will apply to existing businesses with effect from the period of account 1997/98 [*FA 1994, s 211(2)*]. In order to compute the basis period for 1996/97, the old provisions apply. The basis period will normally be for two years or more for the purpose of inclusion of additions and sales, but the calculation of writing down allowance will be based upon the year of assessment, giving one year's claim only.

8.7 For businesses commencing on or after 6 April 1994, the new rules apply immediately. Capital allowances will therefore be calculated based upon the period of account and the resultant allowances deducted from the profits or added to the losses for that period. All references to basis periods for capital allowances are therefore deleted in the legislation.

For examples of periods of account and their relevant writing down allowances in opening years and closing years, see Chapter 6. In the transitional period these are illustrated in Chapter 7, and for a change of accounting date in Chapter 9.

To summarise, businesses that commenced before 6 April 1994 will use the old rules until 1997/98. From the period of account ending in that year, capital allowances and balancing allowances are trading expenses and balancing charges

8.8 Capital Allowances

are trading receipts. Before that time, basis periods are calculated and writing down allowance are only restricted if the assessment is for less than one year. For businesses commencing on or after 6 April 1994, new rules apply from commencement.

A worked example

8.8 Claire commenced trading on 1 May 1994, making up accounts to 31 December. After three years she changed her accounting date to 31 May. She ceased trading on 31 December 1999.

On commencement she owned a car, valued at £8,000 (25% private use). On 30 November 1995 she purchased a computer for £2,000. This machine was part exchanged on 30 April 1997. The selling price was £500 and the replacement cost price was £4,000. She sold her car on 20 September 1998 for £2,600, buying a replacement for £16,000. On cessation her car was valued at £11,500 and the computer at £800.

Her adjusted profits before capital allowances were:

	£
1.5.94 to 31.12.94	6,950
Year ended 1.12.95	12,700
1.1.96 to 31.5.97	23,779
Year ended 31.5.98	14,112
1.6.98 to 31.12.99	11,313

Claire's assessments will be calculated after capital allowances, computed as follows:

	Pool £	Car £		
1.5.94 to 31.12.94				
Introduced		8,000		
WDA (8/12 x 2000)		1,333 less 25% p/u		1,000
		6,667		
Year ended 31.12.95				
Addition	2,000			
WDA	500	1,667 less 25% p/u = 1,250		1,750
	1,500	5,000		
1.1.96 to 31.5.97				
Addition	4,000			
	5,500			
Less Sale	500			
	5,000			
WDA (17/12)	1,771	1,771 less 25% p/u = 1,328		3,099
	3,229	3,229		

Capital Allowances 8.8

Year ended 31.5.98				
WDA	807	807	less 25% p/u = 605	1,412
	2,422	2,422		
Year ended 31.5.99				
Sale		2,600		
Balancing charge		178	less 25% p/u =	134
Addition		16,000		
WDA	606	3,000	less 25% p/u = 2,250	2,856
	1,816	13,000		
1.6.99 to 31.12.99				
Taken over at MV	800	11,500		
Balancing allowance	1,016	1,500	less 25% p/u = 1,125	2,141

Giving profits after capital allowances of:

1.5.94 to 31.12.94	6,950	- 1,000	=	5,950
Year ended 31.12.95	12,700	- 1,750	=	10,950
1.1.96 to 31.5.97	23,779	- 3,099	=	20,680
Year ended 31.5.98	14,112	- 1,412	=	12,700
1.6.98 to 31.12.99	11,313 + 134 -	(2,856 + 2,141)	=	6,450
				56,730

and assessments of:

	£	£
1994/95		
1.5.94 to 31.12.94	5,950	
1.1.95 to 5.4.95		
95/365 x 10950	2,850	8,800
1995/96		
Year ended 31.12.95		10,950
(overlap profits £2,850 overlap period 95 days)		
1996/97		
Year ended 31.5.96		
1.6.95 to 31.12.95		
214/365 x 10,950	6,420	
1.1.96 to 31.5.96		
152/517 x 20,680	6,080	
		12,500
Additional overlap profits		
214 days 1.6.95 to 31.12.95	6,420	
95 days b/f	2,850	
309	9,270	
1997/98		
Year ended 31.5.97		
365/517 x 20,680		14,600

8.8 Capital Allowances

	£	£
1998/99		
Year ended 31.5.98		12,700
1999/2000		
1.6.98 to 31.12.99	6,450	
Less overlap profits b/f	9,270	(2,820)
		56,730

(relievable under *ICTA 1988, s 380* against other income in 1999/2000 or 1998/99).

Notes on Example

1) The basis period for capital allowances will be the same as for the accounts, providing the length of the period of account does not exceed 18 months. Accordingly, the first capital allowance computation is for the eight months to 31 December 1994, notwithstanding the fact that the assessment for 1994/95 is based upon the period to 5 April 1995.

2) It should be noted that the second capital allowance computation is for the year ended 31 December 1995. Accordingly, the addition in November 1995 gives rise to allowances which are taken into account in computing the 1994/95 assessment.

3) Because the accounts for the year ended 31 December 1995 are used in aggregate more than once, allowances are given more than once, but with a corresponding reduction in the overlap profits calculated on that period.

4) Only one capital allowance computation is required for the period 1 January 1996 to 31 May 1997, as the period is 17 months. Accordingly the writing down allowance becomes 17/12ths.

5) The final set of accounts can be for more than 18 months, (and in this case will be taken wholly into the computation of the 1999/2000 assessment). The legislation then provides that where the accounts are made up for more than 18 months for capital allowance purposes, it must be divided into a period of twelve months with a balance period. Accordingly the capital allowance computation will be prepared for the year ended 31 May 1999 and then a final computation for the period 1 June 1999 to 31 December 1999.

6) After computing the capital allowances they are deducted as trading expenses or in the case of the balancing charge treated as a trading receipt to give adjusted profits.

7) Assessments and overlap profits are always calculated on the profits after capital allowances (except transitional overlap reliefs – see 8.2 above).

8) In this example, two overlap profit relief calculations are necessary. The first will be made for the year 1995/96 where the profits for the year ended 31 December 1995 fall into 1994/95 and 1995/96 computation. Because of the change of accounting date, the assessment for 1996/97 will be based upon the new year ending in the fiscal year 1996/97. It is assumed that Claire has given

Capital Allowances 8.8

necessary notice to the Revenue by 31 January 1998. At that stage additional overlap profits are calculated, also based upon the year ended 31 December 1995.

9) The overlap profits are deducted in the final year of assessment, 1999/2000. Note that this gives rise to a loss, even though the accounts show profits for each and every year. The computations can be proved by taking the total profits less capital allowances and comparing with the actual assessments. In total both amount to £56,730.

10) Assuming Claire has no other income, the loss of £2,820 will be relieved against the assessment for 1998/99 by way of an *ICTA 1988, s 380(1)(b)* claim made before 31 January 2002.

Chapter 9

Change of Accounting Date

The objectives of the legislation

9.1 One of the prime objectives of the new legislation is to give complete freedom as to choice of accounting date, both on commencement and during the life of the business. At the same time the Revenue is concerned to ensure that there could be no tax advantage obtained by changing an accounting date. Although the rules introduced are almost neutral, the Revenue has still included anti-avoidance legislation where rapid changes take place (i.e. two changes within five years), unless the later change is made for a bona fide commercial reason.

A period of account of less than twelve months ending in the next fiscal year

9.2 When an accounting date is for a period that is less than twelve months ending in the next fiscal year, then the assessment will be based upon the twelve months ending with the new accounting date [new ICTA 1988, s 62(2)(a) substituted by FA 1994, s 202]. This gives further overlap profits that can be calculated and carried forward for overlap relief [new ICTA 1988, s 63A inserted by FA 1994, s 205]. See the example at 9.8 below.

A period of account of less than twelve months ending in the same fiscal year

9.3 If the accounts are made up to a new accounting date for a period of less than twelve months, and that period falls within the same fiscal year as the previous accounting date, then the old date is ignored and profits are calculated for the longer period of account, i.e. over twelve months to the new accounting date [new ICTA 1988, s 60(5) substituted by FA 1994, s 200]. See the example at 9.9 below.

Overlap relief will be allowed where two periods of account end in the same fiscal year and they are aggregated to form the assessment, see 9.4 below.

A period of account of more than twelve months ending in the next fiscal year

9.4 If the new accounting date is based upon a period of account of more than twelve months, but not more than 18 months, then the whole of the profit of that accounting period will form the basis of assessment of the fiscal year in which the accounts end [new *ICTA 1988, s 62(2)(b)* substituted by *FA 1994, s 202*]. Because the period of account is more than twelve months, writing down allowances will be expanded pro-rata. Overlap relief will then apply [*ICTA 1988, s 63A*]. This is calculated by taking the number of days in the period of account less the number of days in the year of assessment. That proportion of the overlap period relief already available will then be deducted from the profits, or added to the losses of the long period of account. See the example at 9.10 below. For periods of account exceeding 18 months, see 9.12 below.

A period of account of more than twelve months such that there is a fiscal year without accounts

9.5 Where a change of accounting date results in a fiscal year without accounts ending in that year, then the assessment will be based upon the period of twelve months to the new accounting date ending in that year [new *ICTA 1988, s 62(2)(a)(5)*]. The assessment of the next year will be based upon the period of twelve months ending with the new accounting date in that year. The overlap profits will be calculated and will be available to carry forward. See the example at 9.11 below.

Conditions for change of accounting date

9.6 Except in the first three years of trading, it will be necessary to satisfy certain conditions for a change of accounting date to apply. These conditions are set out in *ICTA 1988, s 62A* [inserted by *FA 1994, s 203*].

In order to be a valid change:

(a) the accounting period must not be for a period exceeding 18 months; and
(b) notice must be given to the Revenue by 31 January following the end of the year of assessment in which the new accounting date first falls; and either:
  (i) no change of accounting date has taken place in the five years of assessment preceding the year of change; or
  (ii) the notice of change of date given to the Revenue contains the reason for change and an officer of the Board is satisfied that the changes are made for a bona fide commercial reason. The Revenue have 60 days in which to respond to the notice or else its right of challenge is removed. There is a right of appeal against a refusal by the Revenue to allow the change.

9.7 If the above conditions are not satisfied, then the assessment will be based upon the profits to the old accounting date. Providing the conditions are satisfied in the following fiscal year the change will be deemed to have taken place in the second year to which the new accounting date has been used. The effect of these provisions will be that the overlap relief will be calculated upon the profits of the second, i.e. twelve-month period rather than the first long/short period using the new accounting date.

9.8 Change of Accounting Date

Because of the existence of the change of accounting date rules, a taxpayer will be able to claim credit for overlap profits at any time during the life of the business. This is achieved by extending the accounting period to cover a period of not more than 18 months, or by shortening the period to end in the same fiscal year end as the last year end (providing such a change has not taken place in the five previous years and the relevant notice is given).

During the transitional period any accounting date may be chosen as the profits of the transitional period are averaged. The overlap relief is then calculated on the first assessment under the new rules. That will be the twelve months ending with the new accounting date in the fiscal year 1997/98.

Examples of change of accounting date

A period of account of less than twelve months ending in the next fiscal year

9.8 Colin Davies, who commenced trading on 1 June 1994 and who makes up his accounts to 31 December in each year, decides to change his accounting date to 30 June with effect from 1997. Transitional rules will not apply because Colin Davies commenced after 6 April 1994.

His adjusted profits after capital allowances are:

	£
Year ended 31.12.96	42,000
6 months to 30.6.97	24,000
Year ended 30.6.98	54,000

His overlap profits brought forward are £9,500 with an overlap period of 95 days.

The first year with the new accounting date will be the fiscal year 1997/98. Accordingly his assessments will be:

		£
1996/97 (old date)		
Year ended 31.12.96		42,000
1997/98 (new accounting date)		
12 months ended 30.6.97		
6/12 of 42,000	21,000	
Period to 30.6.97	<u>24,000</u>	45,000
1998/99 (new date)		
Year ended 30.6.98		54,000

As the period from 1 July 1996 to 31 December 1996 (184 days) has been assessed twice, that amount will be added to the overlap profits brought forward as follows:

Change of Accounting Date **9.9**

	Overlap profits	Overlap period
Brought forward	9,500	95 days
1997/98	21,000	184 days
Carried forward	30,500	279 days

In computing the capital allowances for the period to 30 June 1997, only 6/12ths writing down allowance will be available.

A period of account of less than twelve months ending in the same fiscal year

9.9 Doreen Ely, who makes up her accounts to 31 May, decides to change her accounting date to 31 December with effect from 1998.

Her adjusted profits are:

	£
Year ended 31.5.97	30,000
Year ended 31.5.98	35,000
7 months to 31.12.98	7,000
Year ended 31.12.99	48,000

Her overlap profits brought forward are £30,900 with an overlap period of 309 days.

Her assessable profits are:

		£	£	£
1997/98	Year ended 31.5.97			30,000
1998/99	1.6.97 to 31.12.98			
	Year ended 31.5.98	35,000		
	7 months to 31.12.98	7,000	42,000	
	Less overlap profits released		21,400	20,600
1999/2000	Year ended 31.12.99			48,000

As the assessment for 1998/99 is based upon more than twelve months, part of the overlap profits will now be released. This is calculated in the following way:

Number of days in period of account	579
Number of days in year of assessment	365
Number of days released	214

Overlap profits released 214/309 x £30,900 = £21,400

	Overlap profits	Overlap period
Brought forward	30,900	309 days
Released	21,400	214 days
Carried forward	9,500	95 days

9.10 *Change of Accounting Date*

Capital allowances will be calculated separately for each period of account, with 7/12ths writing down allowances given in the period to 31 December 1998.

A period of account of more than twelve months ending in the next fiscal year

9.10 Where accounts are prepared for more than twelve months and a period of account ends in each fiscal year, the basis period is then the period of account. As that period is for more than twelve months overlap relief will be given based upon the number of days in the extended period less the number of days in the year of assessment.

Freda Gray, who has made up her accounts to 30 September for many years, decides to change her accounting date to 31 January.

Her adjusted profits are:

Year ended 30.9.97	£14,000
16 months to 31.1.99	£24,400

Her overlap profits brought forward are £9,350 with an overlap period of 187 days.

Her assessments will be:

	£	£
1997/98 Year ended 30.9.97		14,000
1998/99 16 months to 31.1.99	24,400	
Less overlap relief	6,150	18,250

As the 1998/99 assessment is based on more than twelve months, part of the overlap profits brought forward are released.

Number of days in the period of account	488
Number of days in the year of assessment	365
Number of days released	123

	Overlap profits	Overlap relief
Brought forward	9,350	187
Days released		
123/187 x 9,350	6,150	123
Carried forward	3,200	64

Capital allowances will be based upon the period of account, giving writing down allowances for the 16 months to 31 January 1999 of 16/12ths.

A period of account of more than twelve months such that there is a fiscal year without accounts

9.11 To consider the assessments if the change is for a period of more than twelve months, a further example is required. If the periods of account are

Change of Accounting Date **9.11**

prepared such that there is one fiscal year without any accounts ending in that year then:

(a) the basis period for the fiscal year without an accounting period ending within the fiscal year is the twelve-month period based on the new accounting date ending in that year; and
(b) the basis period for the following tax year is the period of twelve months ending on the new accounting date.

This creates additional overlap profits. Continuing the above example of Doreen Ely:

She subsequently discovers that her new accountancy date is unsatisfactory, as staff are unwilling to undertake stocktaking at the New Year and because of the seasonal nature of her business (sale of Easter eggs) she is holding very high stocks. She gives notice of the proposed change to the Revenue on 30 August 2001, setting out the reason for change and receives clearance for the change.

Her adjusted profits are:

	£
Year ended 31.12.1999	48,000
17 months to 31.5. 2001	103,400

Her overlap profits brought forward are £9,500 with an overlap period of 95 days.

Her assessable profits are:

		£	£
1999/2000	Year ended 31.12.1999		48,000
2000/01	Year ended 31.5.2000		
	1.6.1999 to 31.12.1999 214/365 x 48,000	28,142	
	1.1.2000 to 31.5.2000 152/517 x 103,400	30,400	58,542
2001/02	Year ended 31.5.2001		
	365/517 x 103,400		73,000

	Overlap profits	Overlap period
Brought forward	£9,500	95 days
Overlap 1.6.99 to 31.12.99	£28,142	214
Carried forward	£37,642	309

Capital allowances will be based upon the period of account 1 January 2000 to 31 May 2001 giving 17/12ths writing down allowances.

If the Revenue does not give clearance, the assessment for 2000/01 will be based upon the profits of the year ended 31 December 2000. Doreen Ely can apply again for clearance in 2001/02. If there are five clear years between changes, i.e. first change in 1998/99, next change in 2004/05 or later, then the Revenue's clearance is not required.

9.12 *Change of Accounting Date*

Accounts for more than 18 months

9.12 It would appear that making up accounts for a period in excess of 18 months will not be encouraged by the Revenue. In those circumstances, accounts should be prepared for two periods.

In practice, if accounts are prepared for a period of more than 18 months, then in the fiscal year in which the change takes place the conditions in *ICTA 1988, s 62A* will not be met and the assessment will be based upon the profits of the twelve months ending on the 'old' accounting date. However, if accounts continue to be made up to the 'new' accounting date, then the conditions may well be satisfied in the next fiscal year, or the fiscal year after that.

Example

9.13 Cynthia makes up her accounts to 30 June in each year. She changes her accounting date to 31 March by making up accounts for 21 months to 31 March 2003.

Her basis periods will be:

2001/02   Year ended 30.6.2001
2002/03   Year ended 30.6.2002   (being 12/21 of accounts to 31.3.2003)
2003/04   1.7.2002 to 31.3.2004   (being 9/21 of accounts to 31.3.2003 plus accounts to 31.3.2004)

Overlap relief will be given on 274 days of overlap profits.

Note Capital allowances will be computed for the period:

Year ended 30 June 2002, and 1 July 2002 to 31 March 2003 (9/12 WDA)

with both amounts being deducted from the profits of the 21 months to 31 March 2003 before apportionment.

By comparison, Charles makes up his accounts to 31 December and then changes his accounting date to 30 September by making up accounts for the 21 months to 30 September 2002.

His basis periods will be:

2000/01 Year ended 31.12.2000
2001/02 Year ended 31.12.2001 (being 12/21 of accounts to 30.9.2002)

(*Note* assessment would be based upon the new accounting date (*s 62(5)*). However the first condition in *s 62A* is not satisfied, therefore the old date applies.)

2002/03 Year ended 31.12.2002 (9/21 of accounts to 30.9.2002 plus 3/12 of accounts to 30.9.2003)

(*Note* the accounts ending in the fiscal year are for a period of more than 18 months, therefore the first condition in *s 62A* is not satisfied and the old date is applied.)

2003/04 Year ended 30.9.2003

Note overlap profits computed for the period 1 October 2002 to 31 December 2003 to carry forward.

Failure to give notice

9.14 If notice is not given to the Board by the relevant date, then the adjusted profits after capital allowances for the accounting periods must be apportioned to provide assessments based upon profits to the old accounting date [*ICTA 1988, s 62A(3)*]. Such apportionment will continue until the taxpayer has given notice to the Revenue of the change within the time limit. This will normally mean that for the following fiscal year of assessment the new accounting date will apply.

Chapter 10

Partnerships

Self-assessment with partnership income

10.1 The legislation introduced by the *Finance Act 1994* makes fundamental and far reaching changes to the taxation of partnerships. *ICTA 1988, s 111* previously provided that where two or more people carried on a trade or profession, the income tax was computed for the partnership and they were jointly liable for that tax liability.

10.2 For partnerships commencing on or after 6 April 1994, partnerships changing partners after that date and not making a continuation election, and for existing partnerships from 1997/98, the new *s 111* (as substituted by *FA 1994, s 215*) will apply and the partnership will no longer be assessed to tax. Instead, each individual partner will be responsible for his or her own taxation liability.

10.3 The income of the partnership will still be computed in accordance with the schedules to arrive at the taxable amount for the period of account. For partnerships, a 'period of account' basis will apply to all sources of income, not just trading sources. Therefore, if the partnership has Schedule D Case III or Schedule A income, that amount will be computed on a current year basis, rather than an actual fiscal year basis [new *ICTA 1988, s 111(4)*].

Having arrived at the taxable income under each schedule, that amount is divided between the partners in the profit-sharing ratio of the period of account. The previous concept of dividing the assessable amount in the fiscal year of assessment has been abandoned and, therefore, there will no longer be a mismatch between profits earned and profits taxed with consequential equitable adjustments between the partners.

10.4 The partnership will be responsible for making a return of its income to the Revenue, showing the division of that income between the partners in the partnership statement. The partnership return will also show the name and address and tax reference number of each partner. The partnership should nominate a partner to provide the above information and to agree the taxation liabilities with the Revenue. A binding agreement between the Revenue and that party will bind all of the partners. If the partnership does not nominate a partner, then the Revenue may issue a tax return to any or all of the partners individually.

Any expenditure incurred by a partner on behalf of the partnership must be included in the partnership return. It will not be possible for individual partners to make supplementary claims, whether to expenses or capital allowances, in their own tax returns [Inland Revenue Booklet SAT 1, 5.17].

10.5 The time limit for filing the partnership return will normally be 31 January following the end of the fiscal year of assessment. However, in practice it will be necessary to complete the detail of the partnership return well before that date, to enable the partnership to provide the individual partners with the detail of income from the relevant sources to include in their own personal tax returns. Each individual partner will then be responsible for filing his or her own tax return and paying his or her own tax. The Revenue has indicated that, in the case of large partnerships, it would be prepared to accept payment from the partnership, with a schedule of the division of amounts between the individual partners. Note that in future, each partner will have an individual tax reference and possibly a different tax district.

If the individual partner does not receive the detail of his share of income in time to complete his own tax return, then there will be a penalty, collected from the individual, in respect of the partnership for failure to file a tax return and also penalties in respect of the individuals' own failure to file by the due date. It may therefore be appropriate, in the case of large or difficult partnerships, to have an accounting date early in the fiscal year, so that more time is available to agree the accounts and the division of partnership profits.

New partners

10.6 When the new system is in force, each partner will be taxed individually. Therefore, when a person joins a partnership, he must estimate his share of profits from the date of commencement to the following 5 April and include that estimate in his personal tax return. If the partnership makes up its accounts to a date early in the fiscal year, then the actual figures will be available and no estimates will be required.

Example

10.7 Joan becomes a partner in Books For All on 1 June 1998. Books For All has made up its accounts to 30 April for many years.

First year of assessment (for Joan) – 1998/99

Joan will be assessed on her profits from 1 June 1998 to 5 April 1999 (being part of the accounts for the year ended 30 April 1999).

The above amount must be included in her tax return for 1998/99, which must be filed by 31 January 2000. Joan will hopefully have an agreed profit figure for the year ended 30 April 1999 before she needs to file her tax return.

Second year of assessment (for Joan) – 1999/2000

10.8 *Partnerships*

As Joan has only been a partner since 1 June 1998, her period of account is effectively 1 June 1998 to 30 April 1999. As this period is less than twelve months, she will be assessed upon the profits of her first twelve months of trading.

Joan is therefore assessed upon the period 1 June 1998 to 31 May 1999. In order to compute her assessments, she will need the accounts for the year ended 30 April 2000, but as her tax return for 1999/2000 does not have to be filed until 31 January 2001, this information should be available by the due date.

Joan will compute overlap profits for the period 1 June 1998 to 5 April 1999. That overlap relief will be personal to Joan.

Third year of assessment (for Joan) – 2000/01

Joan will now be assessed on the period of account for the year ended 30 April 2000, i.e. in line with all other partners. The accounts for the year ended 30 April 2000 forms the basis of assessment for 2000/01, with a latest filing date of 31 January 2002.

By comparison, if a partnership makes up its accounts to a date late in the fiscal year estimates will be needed and time limits will become tight.

Example

10.8 Trevor becomes a member of the partnership of Bookbrowse on 1 June 1998. Bookbrowse has made up its accounts to 28 February for many years.

First year of assessment (for Trevor) – 1998/99

Trevor will be assessed upon the profits for the period 1 June 1998 to 5 April 1999. This will require the accounts for the year ended 28 February 1999 and also the accounts for the year ended 28 February 2000.

Trevor is obliged to file his tax return for 1998/99 by 31 January 2000 and yet the accounts needed to compute the assessable profits do not end until 28 February 2000, hence the need for estimate and payments on account which, if incorrect, will give rise to a charge to interest.

Second year of assessment (for Trevor) – 1999/2000

Trevor will have a period of account being the year ended 28 February 2000, i.e. the same period of account as the other partners. The tax return for 1999/2000 must be filed by 31 January 2001.

Trevor will compute overlap profits for the period 1 March 1999 to 5 April 1999 to carry forward for his individual use.

In the second example there are eleven months in which to prepare accounts, agree the division of profits and file any individual returns, whereas in the first example there are 21 months available to agree the accounting information.

Retirement of a partner

10.9 Similar principles will apply on the retirement of a partner. The final assessment will be based upon the period from the accounting date ending in the preceding fiscal year to the date of cessation in the final year. From that amount will be deducted the overlap profits of that individual.

Example

10.10 Joan from the above example ceases to be a partner on 31 December 2002. Books For All still makes up its accounts for the year ended 30 April.

Penultimate year (for Joan) – 2001/02

Based upon the year ended 30 April 2001

Year of cessation (for Joan) 2002/03

Joan will be assessed upon her share of profits for the year ended 30 April 2002 plus her share of profits for the period 1 May 2002 to 31 December 2002 less the overlap profits brought forward.

In order to compute her assessment, accounts for the year ended 30 April 2003 will be required. As the filing date for 2002/03 is 31 January 2004, this information should be available by the filing date.

By comparison, if Trevor in example 10.8 above ceases to trade on 31 March 2003, his assessments will be:

Penultimate year (for Trevor) – 2001/02

Trevor will be assessed upon his share of profits based upon the year ended 28 February 2002.

Year of cessation (for Trevor) – 2002/03

Trevor will be assessed upon his share of profits for the year ended 28 February 2003 plus his share of profits for the period of 1 March 2003 to 31 March 2003. Therefore accounts for the year ended 28 February 2004 will be required to complete the 2002/03 tax return, which must be filed by 31 January 2004.

The above difficulty will only arise if a partner ceases to trade after the normal accounting date but within the fiscal year, i.e. in the case of Trevor above he has ceased trading after 28 February 2003 but before 5 April 2003. Again estimates will be required and if they prove to be incorrect interest will be charged on any underpayments or paid (at a lower rate) on any overpayments.

The continuing partners

10.11 Because assessments are no longer based upon the partnership profits,

10.12 *Partnerships*

but on the individual's own share, there is no longer any possibility of a continuation election under the new rules. Each partner is dealt with as an individual, having opening year rules when he or she joins and applying the closing year provisions with overlap relief on cessation.

Change of partner before 5 April 1997

10.12 For existing businesses that cease after 6 April 1994 but before 5 April 1997, continuation elections will still be available and the old rules will then apply. If the partners do not sign a continuation election under *ICTA 1988, s 113(2)*, then there will be a deemed cessation and the old rules will apply to the previous partnership and the new rules will apply to the new partnership.

In the circumstances where profits are declining, so that there will not be a revision to actual on the application of old cessation rules, then no continuation election should be made, thus using the new rules at an earlier stage. The comparison will be the period of dropout applicable under cessation rules compared with the period of dropout under transitional rules. Whichever average profit is higher should be allowed to drop out of account.

The transitional period

10.13 For partnerships trading before 6 April 1994 and still trading after 5 April 1997, the normal transitional rules apply (see Chapter 7). Therefore in 1996/97 the profits of the accounts on the preceding year basis for that year plus the profits for the current year basis for that year are aggregated and 365/731 of that figure is taken as the assessable amount. For 1997/98, the current year basis applies and the profits after capital allowances of the accounting period ending in that year forms the basis of assessment.

The transitional overlap relief is calculated for the period of time before 5 April 1997 included in the 1997/98 assessment based upon the adjusted profits before capital allowances. That overlap relief is divided between the partners for use by them when they leave the partnership. Just as the assessable profits of the partnership for 1997/98 are divided between the partners in their profit-sharing ratio for the period of account, the overlap profit relief will be divided between the partners in accordance with their profit-sharing ratio for the period of overlap.

Overlap relief is also calculated for all other sources of income as though it were the income of a second deemed trade (see 10.22 below).

Example

10.14 The Peter partnership has traded for many years, making up its accounts to 31 December in each year.

Its adjusted profits (before capital allowances) are:

Partnerships **10.15**

	Profits	Capital allowances
	£	£
Year ended 31.12.95	30,100 ⎫	2,500
Year ended 31.12.96	43,000 ⎭	
Year ended 31.12.97	50,000	2,000

The partners Peter and Paul share profits 60%:40% until 31 March 1997, when profit shares become equal.

The assessable profits will be:

			£	£
1996/97	Year ended 31.12.95		30,100	
	Year ended 31.12.96		43,000	
		365/731 x	73,100	36,500
	Less capital allowances 1996/97			
	(Basis Period 1.1.95 to 31.12.96)			2,500
				34,000
	Divided			
	Peter – 60%		20,400	
	Paul – 40%		13,600	
1997/98	Year ended 31.12.97		50,000	
	Less capital allowances		2,000	48,000

	Divided	Total	Peter	Paul
1.1.97 to 31.3.97	60:40	11,836	7,102	4,734
1.4.97 to 31.12.97	50:50	36,164	18,082	18,082
		48,000	25,184	22,816

With overlap profits computed as follows:

Profits before capital allowances for year ended 31.12.97 = £50,000

	Total	Peter	Paul
90/365 x £50,000 to 31.3.97	12,329	7,397	4,932
5/365 x £50,000 to 5.4.97	685	343	342
	13,014	7,740	5,274

Current year basis – a worked example

10.15 The current year basis of assessment rules for a partnership work in exactly the same way as for individuals. That is to say, the profits that will be

85

10.16 *Partnerships*

assessed over the life of the partnership are exactly the same as the profits shown in the accounts (adjusted for disallowable items). In addition, the profits of each individual partner over the life of the partnership will normally be the share allocated to the partner in the accounts. The previous adjustments that arose where the partnership made a profit but an individual partner's share was a loss or vice versa are retained [Inland Revenue Booklet SAT 1, 5.23].

Example

10.16 The Quarum partnership commenced trading on 1 August 1994, making up its accounts to 30 June each year. The original partners shared profits:

Kim   50%
Abbie   50%

On 1 July 1998 Julia joined the firm which adopted a revised profit share of 40:40:20.

On 30 June 2000 Kim ceased to be a partner, Abbie and Julia then sharing profits 75%:25%. The business ceased on 31 March 2001.

The adjusted profits (after capital allowances) are:

	£
1 August 1994 to 30 June 1995	24,200
Year ended 30 June 1996	18,000
Year ended 30 June 1997	30,000
Year ended 30 June 1998	26,000
Year ended 30 June 1999	48,000
Year ended 30 June 2000	12,000
1 July 2000 to 31 March 2001	8,000
	166,200

The profits assessable on the partners would be:

	Total	Kim	Abbie	Julia
	£	£	£	£
1994/95				
248/334 x £24,200	17,968	8,984	8,984	
1995/96 (Y/E 31.7.95)				
1.8.94 to 30.6.95	24,200			
1.7.95 to 31.7.95				
31/365 x 18,000	1,528			
	25,728	12,864	12,864	
1996/97				
Y/E 30.6.96	18,000	9,000	9,000	

Partnerships **10.16**

	Total £	Kim £	Abbie £	Julia £
Overlap profits:				
248 days to 5.4.95	17,968	8,984	8,984	
31 days to 31.7.95	1,528	764	764	
279	19,496	9,748	9,748	
1997/98				
Y/E 30.6.97	30,000	15,000	15,000	
1998/99				
Y/E 30.6.98	26,000	13,000	13,000	
1.7.98 to 5.4.99				
279/365 x 9,600	7,338			7,338
	33,338			

(i.e. take Julia's profit share per accounts 48,000 x 20% = 9,600 proportioned to the fiscal year)

1999/2000				
Y/E 30.6.99	48,000	19,200	19,200	9,600
Overlap profits				
279 days 1.7.98 to 5.4.99				(7,338)
2000/01				
Y/E 30.6.2000		4,800	4,800	2,400

On Kim – profits to cessation		4,800		
Less overlap profits		(9,748)		
Loss		(4,948)		

On Abbie and Julia
Share to 30.6.2000

			Abbie	Julia
			4,800	2,400
To cessation (75:25)			6,000	2,000
			10,800	4,400
Less overlap profits			(9,748)	(7,338)
			1,052	(2,938)

(Although Kim and Julia have losses available for relief and Abbie has an assessable profit, no further adjustment is needed. This is because the losses are due to overlap relief and *not* because of the allocation of shares of profits.)

10.17 Partnerships

Summary of assessments

	Total £	Kim £	Abbie £	Julia £
1994/95	17,968	8,984	8,984	
1995/96	25,728	12,864	12,864	
1996/97	18,000	9,000	9,000	
1997/98	30,000	15,000	15,000	
1998/99	33,338	13,000	13,000	7,338
1999/2000	48,000	19,200	19,200	9,600
2000/01	(6,834)	(4,948)	1,052	(2,938)
	166,200	73,100	79,100	14,000

It will be noted above that the total profits assessed are £166,200, being the amount of the adjusted profits after capital allowances. In the year 2000/01 Abbie has a profit of £1,052 whereas Kim and Julia both show losses. Kim and Julia are able to claim loss relief in their own names and therefore to make a personal choice as to the way in which that loss is relieved.

Not only does the partnership pay tax on precisely the same figures as it earned, but each individual partner also is assessed on the profits allocated to them in the accounts.

Summary of division of accounting profits

	Total £	Kim £	Abbie £	Julia £
1 August 1994 to 30 June 1995	24,200	12,100	12,100	–
Year ended 30 June 1996	18,000	9,000	9,000	–
Year ended 30 June 1997	30,000	15,000	15,000	–
Year ended 30 June 1998	26,000	13,000	13,000	–
Year ended 30 June 1999	48,000	19,200	19,200	9,600
Year ended 30 June 2000	12,000	4,800	4,800	2,400
1 July 2000 to 31 March 2001	8,000	–	6,000	2,000
	166,200	73,100	79,100	14,000

10.17 However, this does not mean to say that the tax liability will be the same under a current year basis as under an actual basis. For example in the above division of accounting profits all partners make profits in all accounting periods and yet for taxation purposes there are losses for Kim and Julia in 2000/01. This is because of the duplication of profits in earlier years which are carried forward, in this example, to a period of time in which profits are lower. Because of the need to offset losses fully against other income under *ICTA 1988, s 380,* or fully against profits under *ICTA 1988, s 385,* it may be that the losses will not be effectively relieved, whereas the profits may be chargeable at basic or higher rates.

There is still the effect that tax will be paid in arrears because it is based upon the profits of the accounting period which may be as much as 11 months 29 days out of step with the financial year. If profits are rising then the duplication in earlier years is likely to result in a duplication of lower profits and therefore

Partnerships **10.19**

be cash flow advantageous in all years except the last. In the same way, if profits are falling, to have an accounting date early in the financial year would mean duplication of high profits with no relief until cessation and the consequential cash flow loss. For most partnerships who are unable to forecast profits accurately for the foreseeable future the overriding practical need will be to have information available at an early stage. The ability to achieve compliance with tax return time limits is likely to outweigh unknown changes in profits in future years.

A practical solution could be to prepare accounts to 5 April after commencement and also to 30 April after commencement. Before those figures are submitted to the Revenue a trend of profits for the coming twelve months would be known. If profits are rising then accounts could be submitted to 30 April, whereas if profits are falling the accounts to 5 April would be used.

Partnerships assessed on an actual basis in 1995/96

10.18 If an existing partnership has had a change of personal before 5 April 1994 and has not made a *ICTA 1988, s 113(2)* election for the continuation basis, then *ICTA 1988, s 61(4)* applies so that the actual basis is used for the first four years of assessment. If the partnership change occurred during 1993/94 then actual basis will apply for that year and the three following years. There will be no transitional year in 1996/97. New rules will then apply for 1997/98 with overlap profit relief being calculated in the normal way.

Example

10.19 The Rudge partnership has a change of partners on 30 September 1993 and no election was made for continuation basis to apply.

The adjusted profits before capital allowances are:

	£
Year ended 30.9.94	27,375
Year ended 30.9.95	29,200
Year ended 30.9.96	28,548
Year ended 30.9.97	36,500

Capital allowances are:

	£
1993/94 Year ended 5.4.94	2,250
1994/95 Year ended 5.4.95	3,310
1995/96 Year ended 5.4.96	3,120
1996/97 Year ended 5.4.97	2,640

For the accounting period to 30 September 1997, the new rules apply and additions/sales for the period 6 April 1997 to 30 September 1997 are taken into account together with the carried forward amount at 5 April 1997. One full year's writing down allowance applies.

10.20 *Partnerships*

Where there is an overlap of two periods of account the common period is deemed to fall in the first period of account only [new *CAA 1990, s 160(3)(a)* substituted by *FA 1994, s 212*].

Assume that the computed capital allowances for 1997/98 amount to £2,920.

Actual basis will apply because of *ICTA 1988, s 61(4)* (old rules).

			£
1993/94			
187/365 x 27,375	14,025 - 2,250	=	11,775
1994/95			
178/365 x 27,375 = 13,350			
187/365 x 29,200 = <u>14,960</u>	28,310 - 3,310	=	25,000
1995/96			
178/365 x 29,200 = 14,240			
188/366 x 28,548 = <u>14,664</u>	28,904 - 3,120	=	25,784
1996/97			
178/366 x 28,548 = 13,884			
187/365 x 36,500 = <u>18,700</u>	32,584 - 2,640	=	29,944

Under the new rules the current year basis applies:

	£
1997/98	
Y/E 30.9.97 (36,500 - 2,920)	33,580
With overlap profits of	
187/365 x 36,500	18,700

The overlap profits will be divided between the partners in their profit sharing ratio of the period 1 October 1996 to 5 April 1997.

10.20 If the partnership change occurred before 6 April 1993 then normal transitional rules will apply with the option of the taxpayer to revise the fifth and sixth year of assessment to actual. Should the transitional year be the sixth year then the assessments will be as for the Rudge partnership above, that is to say actual until 1996/97 and current year basis thereafter. The same will effectively happen if 1996/97 is the fifth year and an election has been made under *ICTA 1988, s 62* for actual basis (see also the notes and example at 7.15 above where the 1995/96 assessment is based upon the profits of the year ended 5 April 1996 (actual basis)).

Corporate partners

10.21 If a partnership has a corporate partner, then its share of profits are computed as if the partnership is a corporation. Accordingly, if the accounting period of the company differs from that of the partnership, the company's share of partnership profits will be apportioned on a time basis to the chargeable accounting periods of the company. Capital allowances are computed separately, as for a corporation tax computation, and are allocated between the corporate and non-corporate partners. Those allowances are then relieved in the relevant chargeable accounting periods of the company and are deducted from the profits of the individuals for the period of account.

Income other than Schedule D Case I/II

10.22 All income of a partnership is to be assessed using the same basis periods. Where a partnership has Case I/II income then the basis period will be that of the trading income. This will apply even where the trading income is a minor part of the partnership business [Inland Revenue Booklet SAT 1, 5.34].

Where a partnership commences, or a new partner joins an existing partnership and that partnership has untaxed income from one or more sources then all of those sources are aggregated and are deemed to be a second trade or profession. Overlap relief is computed in accordance with the normal rules for trades.

Where such overlap relief has been computed then it will be relieved on a change of accounting date or on cessation. Note it is the cessation of being a partner that gives overlap relief not the cessation of the source of other income. Accordingly it is possible that there is no other income at the time the overlap is available. It is therefore provided that if the relief exceeds the other income the excess shall be deducted from the individual's other income for the year of cessation (or change of accounting date). [New *ICTA 1988, s 111* substituted by *FA 1995, s 117*].

If a partnership does not have any income chargeable under Schedule D Case I/II then the computational rules that apply are those for an individual with Schedule D Case III income.

Chapter 11

Losses

Fiscal year basis in practice

11.1 Under existing legislation, relief for trading losses is technically given on an actual basis. In practice, the strict basis is not always used and instead loss relief is given on a basis equivalent to a current year basis. That is to say, relief is given for the loss of the accounts ending in the fiscal year as opposed to apportioning losses over fiscal years. However, the strict basis always applies to the opening and closing years of a business and where the taxpayer has elected for that basis. A further complication is that capital allowances are dealt with separately, adding to the number of options for relief.

11.2 The present rules will continue to apply to businesses trading on 5 April 1994 for the years of assessment up to and including 1995/96. Special rules will apply for the year 1996/97. Relief in that year is against total income for 1996/97 or 1995/96. The time limit for claim in that year is twelve months after 31 January following the end of the fiscal year, i.e. 31 January 1999. To ensure that full relief is given for losses they are treated as nil in the transitional calculation, but granted in full in the loss relief claim. If the loss was included in the normal transitional calculation, then one half or more of those losses could be effectively lost. The new rules will apply to businesses that commenced on or after 6 April 1994 from that time.

Loss relief under current year basis

11.3 Under the new rules, the same principles will apply to the calculation of a loss as to the calculation of a trading profit. This means that capital allowances will become trading expenses, with balancing charges treated as trading receipts [new *ICTA 1988, s 382(3)* substituted by *FA 1994, s 209(3)*]. Although this will simplify the loss relief claim, it does mean that it will be necessary to consider fully the usage of the losses before finalising the claim for capital allowances. It will still be possible to disclaim or restrict claims for capital allowances, thus giving an opportunity to minimise the loss of personal reliefs where a loss claim is made.

11.4 Because trading losses are treated in the same way as trading profits, they can be used in the calculation of two years of assessment using the same basis period rules as apply for profits. If an overlap in basis periods occurs, then loss relief is to be given in the earlier of the periods only [new *ICTA 1988, s 382(4)* substituted by *FA 1994, s 209(3)*].

11.5 Special rules will continue to apply to losses arising during the first four years of assessment [*ICTA 1988, s 381*]. Any unrelieved losses will be carried forward for relief against future trading profits from the same source [*ICTA 1988, s 385*]. On cessation it will still be possible to carry losses backwards for three years under terminal loss relief [*ICTA 1988, s 388*].

11.6 From 1996/97 the time limit for loss relief claims are amended and become one year from the 31 January following the year of assessment for *s 380* claims and five years from 31 January following the year of assessment for *s 385* and *s 388* claims. The time limit for *s 381* claims remains at two years from the end of the fiscal year in which the loss was incurred. In most instances the time limits will therefore be shortened by approximately nine weeks.

Relief for trading losses against other income

11.7 Under existing legislation, relief for trading losses will be given against income from other sources for the year of loss and the year following the year of loss, providing the trade is carried on in that following year. The relief is given against the full amount of income for the year of claim, restricted only by the availability of loss. Any balance is then available in the other year.

If the claim is made for a year other than the year of loss then, when the relief has been computed in terms of a reduction in tax (and Class 4 NIC) liability of the earlier year, that amount is claimed as a reduction of tax payable for the year of loss, any excess being repaid by 31 January following the end of the fiscal year of loss [*TMA 1970, s 42(3A)* introduced by *FA 1995, s 107*].

11.8 Under the new legislation relief for trading losses will be given against other income of the year of loss, or against income of the year preceding the year of loss [new *ICTA 1988, s 380(1)(2)* substituted by *FA 1994, s 209(1)*]. As with the current relief, the claim will not be restricted but will be against the full amount of other income, limited only by the availability of loss.

A claim may be made for:

(a) relief against income of the year of loss; or
(b) relief against income of the preceding year of loss; or
(c) relief against income of the year of loss with the balance carried back against the income of the preceding year; or
(d) relief against income of the preceding year of loss with the balance carried forward against the income of the year of loss.

Any unrelieved loss will then be carried forward against profits from the same source in future years.

The Treasury notes indicate that the taxpayer has a right to claim loss relief under *ICTA 1988, s 380(1)(b)* against total income of the previous year and then to carry any unrelieved loss forward to the year of loss itself making a claim under *ICTA*

11.9 *Losses*

1988, s 380(1)(a). If there are two loss claims available for any given year then *ICTA 1988, s 380(2)* provides that a loss is set off against general income for the year of loss in priority to a claim brought backward to a year.

As the loss is after the inclusion of capital allowances, there is no longer a need to specifically add capital allowances to the loss claim and therefore *ICTA 1988, s 383* is repealed [*FA 1994, s 214(1)(b)*].

11.9 The time limit for making a *s 380* loss claim remains at two years from the end of the fiscal year in which the loss was incurred, until 1996/97. Then the time limit becomes twelve months after 31 January following the end of the tax year in which the loss was incurred, e.g. relief for 1996/97 must be claimed by 31 January 1999.

Example

11.10 James King (who is single) makes up his accounts to 30 September each year and has the following income:

Schedule D I   Including capital allowances of

	£	£
Year ended 30.9.97 Profit	8,000	900
Year ended 30.9.98 Loss	(4,975)	675
Year ended 30.9.99 Profit	4,700	500

Other income

	£
1997/98	4,700
1998/99	3,200
1999/2000	2,600

Assume a personal allowance of £3,525 for each year.

His assessment for 1997/98 would originally be:

	£
Schedule D Case I	8,000
Other income	4,700
	12,700
Personal allowance	3,525
	9,175

For 1998/99:

Schedule D Case I	Loss
Other income	3,200
	3,200
Personal allowance	3,525
	NIL

Available for *s 380* loss relief:

Schedule D I (y/e 30.9.98)   (4,975)

This is available in 1998/99 or 1997/98 and the claim must be made by 31 January 2001.

James claims in 1997/98, giving a revised assessment of:

	£
Schedule D I	8,000
Other income	4,700
	12,700
Less *s 380* loss relief	4,975
	7,725
Less personal allowance	3,525
	4,200

James in theory could have claimed relief of £3,200 in 1998/99, carrying the balance of £1,775 back to 1997/98. As the effect would merely be to increase the unrelieved personal allowances, this would be a pointless claim. In the same way, capital allowances could have been disclaimed but in this example it would not benefit James to do so. Alternatively James could have carried the loss forward against future profits from the same source under *ICTA 1988, s 385*. This is illustrated at 11.16 below.

Relief for trading losses in opening years

11.11 Special relief for trading losses in the first three tax years of a trade, profession or vocation continues to be available [*ICTA 1988, s 381*]. The available loss relief is calculated using the same basis period rules as for trading profits. If a loss appears in more than one calculation then it is not included in the computation for the second year. Therefore the use of an accounting date other than 5 April restricts the period of loss available for claim under this section.

In the year of commencement and the three following years of assessment losses computed can therefore be relieved under *s 380* against other income of the year of loss or of the preceding year; or, under *s 381*, against the total income of the taxpayer of the year three years before the year to which the loss relates. Relief is given to the full extent of total income for that earlier year and is then carried forward against other income of the following years. Relief is given for the earliest year in preference to the later years.

11.12 In order to claim relief under this section it is necessary to show that the trade was carried on on a commercial basis with a view to profits and that profits can be reasonably expected within a reasonable time thereafter [*ICTA 1988, s 381(4)*].

The time limit for claim remains as two years after the end of the fiscal year to which the loss relates.

11.13 Losses

The reduction in tax computed for the earlier year is given as a deduction against the tax liability of the year in which the loss was incurred.

Example

11.13 Karen Long commenced trading on 1 November 1994 making up her accounts to 30 September in each year. She has other income of £1,000 p.a., was previously employed at £12,000 p.a. and is entitled to a single allowance.

Her accounts show the following (assume no claims for capital allowances):

	£	£
1.11.94 to 30.9.95	(33,000)	
Year ended 30.9.96	2,400	
Year ended 30.9.97	48,000	

Schedule D I assessments (without loss relief):

1994/95 1.11.94 to 5.4.95		NIL
Loss available:		
Loss 5/11 x £33,000	15,000	
1995/96 1.11.94 to 31.10.95		
Loss 1.11.94 to 30.9.95	(33,000)	
Less included in 1994/95	15,000	
	(18,000)	
Profit 1.10.94 to 31.10.95		
1/12 x £2,400	200	
Loss available	(17,800)	NIL
1996/97 year ended 30.9.96		2,400
1997/98 year ended 30.9.97		48,000

With overlap profits of £200 and overlap period of 31 days.

Note, the actual overlap periods are 1 November 1994 to 5 April 1995 and 1 October 1995 to 31 October 1995, but where a loss is included in two periods then it is excluded from the second period in computing the overlap profit relief [*ICTA 1988, s 63A(4)*]. Therefore, the overlap profits will only be for the period 1 October 1995 to 31 October 1995. The overlap period is defined as being, in relation to an overlap profit, the numbers of days in the period in which the overlap profit arose [*ICTA 1988, s 63A(5)*].

It is therefore considered that the overlap period would only be 31 days in the above example. This could mean that on cessation Karen Long would have profits based, for example, on the year ended 30 September having only been in self-employment for the period 6 April to 30 September. Normally this will

Losses **11.13**

be counteracted by a deduction of overlap profits representing a period of approximately six months. Because of the loss relief claims in opening years Karen would only have a deduction for 31 days. This could give unexpected and unpleasant results on cessation.

As an alternative to relief under *s 380* Karen Long has the possibility of making a claim under *s 381* against total income of the three years preceding the year of loss, these claims would be as follows:

	£
Trading loss of 1994/95 available for relief	(15,000)

Available under *ICTA 1988, s 381* in:
    (i) 1991/92 (with balance carried forward to)
    (ii) 1992/93
    (iii) 1993/94

Giving claims of:

	£	£	£
1991/92 Schedule E	12,000		
Other income	1,000	13,000	
1994/95 *s 381* claim		(13,000)	NIL
Loss available		(15,000)	
Loss used		13,000	
Loss carried forward		(2,000)	
1992/93 Schedule E	12,000		
Other income	1,000	13,000	
Balance of 1994/95 *s 381* claim		(2,000)	11,000

Time limit for claim being 5 April 1997.

If the above claims were made, personal allowances would be lost in 1991/92 but a repayment supplement would be made on the tax repayment for that year. The balance of loss for 1995/96 could then be relieved under *s 380* as above, or under *s 381*, as follows:

Trading loss of 1995/96 available for relief	(17,800)

Available in:
    (i) 1992/93 (with balance carried forward)
    (ii) 1993/94
    (iii) 1994/95

Giving claims of:

11.14 *Losses*

1992/93 total income as above	11,000	
1995/96 *s 381* claim	(11,000)	NIL
Loss available for relief	(17,800)	
Claimed 1992/93	11,000	
Loss carried forward to 1993/94	(6,800)	
1993/94 Schedule E	12,000	
Other income	1,000	
	13,000	
Balance of *s 381* claim	(6,800)	
		6,200

If the above *s 381* claim was made, personal allowances would be lost fully in 1992/93 and partially in 1993/94.

Relief for national insurance

11.14 If loss claims are made either under *s 380* or *s 381* against other income then for Class 4 National Insurance purposes a loss is calculated to be carried forward to relieve profits from the trading source. Accordingly, regardless of the claims made above, for Class 4 purposes the unrelieved loss as at 5 April 1996 would be £32,800 being the loss of £33,000 less £200 used in overlap. This would be relieved against the first available profits from the same trade, i.e.

1996/97	£2,400
1997/98	£30,400

Therefore the income for Class 4 National Insurance purposes in 1997/98 would be:

Schedule D Case I assessment	£48,000
NIC Class 4 loss	£30,400
Class 4 profits for year	£17,600

Relief for trading losses carried forward

11.15 Insofar as trading losses are not offset against other income, relief will be available, by claim, against future profits from the same source [*ICTA 1988, s 385*]. The time limit for the claim is five years after the 31 January following the year of loss. In practice, such loss relief claims are made by way of income tax computations.

Example

11.16 James King (who is single) makes up his accounts to 30 September each year and has the following income:

Schedule D I

	£	Including capital allowances of £
Year ended 30.9.97 Profit	8,000	900
Year ended 30.9.98 Loss	(4,975)	675
Year ended 30.9.99 Profit	4,700	1,000

Other Income

	£
1997/98	4,700
1998/99	3,200
1999/2000	2,600

Assume a personal allowance of £3,525 for each year.

If James King decided not to make a *s 380* claim, but to carry losses forward against future profits from the same source under *s 385*, then his assessments would be:

	£	£
1997/98 Schedule D Case I		8,000
1998/99 Schedule D Case I		NIL
1999/2000 Schedule D Case I	4,700	
Less loss b/f	4,975	
Loss c/f	275	
Other income	2,600	
Less personal allowance	3,525	NIL

In practice, the unrelieved personal allowances could be retrieved by restricting the capital allowance claims in the year to 30 September 1998. This could be done by repairing the tax return for the year to 5 April 1999. The filing date for that tax return would be 31 January 2000, giving a time limit on repairing claims of the period to 31 January 2001. If the capital allowances in the year ended 30 September 1998 were restricted to nil, there would be a revised loss claim of £4,300. As this would still leave unrelieved allowances, it would then be necessary to restrict the capital allowance claim for the year to 30 September 1999 as well to say £475, giving a revised assessment of:

	£	£
Profits before capital allowances	5,700	
Less revised capital allowances	475	
Schedule D Case I profits		5,225
Less loss b/f (y/e 30.9.98)		4,300
		925
Other income		2,600
		3,525
Less personal allowance		3,525
		NIL

11.17 *Losses*

Relief for terminal losses

11.17 Where a trading loss is incurred in the last twelve months of the life of a business, then special relief is available. The relief is calculated by taking the loss of the actual period of the final twelve months. Such a loss is then relieved against trading profits, if any, of the fiscal year of cessation and of the three preceding fiscal years (giving relief against later years in preference to earlier years) [*ICTA 1988, s 388*]. The time limit for claiming terminal loss relief will be five years from 31 January following the fiscal year of cessation. Insofar as any of the loss would relate to the year of assessment preceding the ultimate year, then the time limit will be based upon that earlier year.

Example

11.18 Norah Otter ceased trading on 5 April 2001. Her adjusted profits were:

	£
Year ended 5.4.1998	12,000
Year ended 5.4.1999	6,000
Year ended 5.4.2000	2,000
Year ended 5.4.2001 – Loss	(11,000)

She has no other income.

As the fiscal year basis applies there is no overlap profit relief.

Her terminal loss claim will be:

	£	
2000/01 – Year ended 5.4.2001		(11,000)

Offset against profits of same trade:	
1999/2000	2,000
1998/1999	6,000
1997/1998 (balance)	3,000
	11,000

Giving a revised 1997/98 assessment of:	
Profit	12,000
Loss relief *s 388*	(3,000)
	9,000

With a claim required by 31 January 2007.

Example

11.19 In computing assessable profits or losses, overlap profit relief is treated as a deduction.

Oliver Patel ceased trading on 30 June 2001. His adjusted profits (losses) have been:

Losses **11.20**

	£
Year ended 31.12.1998	15,000
Year ended 31.12.1999	12,000
Year ended 31.12.2000	14,000
Period ended 30.6.2001 – Loss	(9,700)

With overlap profits brought forward of £5,800.

He has no other income.

His assessment for 2001/2002 would be nil, i.e.

	£	£
2001/02 – 6 months to 30.6.2001		(9,700)
Overlap profits relief		(5,800)
		(15,500)

and his terminal loss claim would be:

	£	£
Adjusted loss for period of		
6 months 1.1.2001 to 30.6.2001		(15,500)
6 months 1.7.2000 to 31.12.2000		NIL
		(15,500)
Available in 2000/01	14,000	
1999/2000 (balance)	1,500	

Giving assessments of:

2000/01	NIL
1999/2000 (12,000 - 1,500)	10,500
1998/99	15,000

11.20 Terminal loss relief will be given after normal loss relief against other income. Where a loss is incurred in the penultimate period then it may well only partially fall into a terminal loss claim. This again will give the taxpayer a choice of ways in which loss relief claims can be made. In computing profits for Class 4 National Insurance it must be remembered that any loss claim against other income will form a separate loss relief to carry forward for Class 4 purposes only.

If the adjusted results of Oliver had been:

	£
Year ended 31.12.1998	15,000
Year ended 31.12.1999	12,000
Year ended 31.12.2000	(9,700)
Period ended 30.6.2001	14,000

With overlap profits brought forward of £5,800 and no other income his assessments would then be:

11.20 *Losses*

	£	£
1998/99 (year ended 31.12.1998)		15,000
1999/2000 (year ended 31.12.1999)	12,000	
Less s 380 loss relief	9,700	2,300
2000/01 (year ended 31.12.2000)		NIL
2001/02 – 6 months to 30.6.2001	14,000	
Less overlap profits	5,800	8,200

If it was decided not to make a claim under *s 380* to carry the relief back for the year ended 31 December 2000 to the year 1999/2000 then the relief would normally be carried forward under *s 385*. Insofar as relief was not available under *s 385* then a terminal loss relief claim would be possible. Continuing the above example with *s 385* relief and then *s 388* relief the assessments would be:

	£	£
1998/99 (year ended 31.12.1998)		15,000
1999/2000 (year ended 31.12.1999)	12,000	
Less terminal loss relief (*s 388*)	1,500	10,500
2000/01 (year ended 31.12.2000)		NIL
2001/02 6 months to 30.6.2001	14,000	
Less overlap profits	(5,800)	
	8,200	
Less unused losses b/f (*s 385*)	(9,700)	NIL
Unrelieved losses	(1,500)	

Loss of last 12 months:

6 months to 30.6.2001 (Profit £8200)		NIL
Loss of 6 months to 31.12.2000		
1/2 x £9,700 =	4,850	
restricted to unrelieved loss	1,500	
s 388 loss		1,500

Available in:

2001/02	NIL
2000/01	NIL
1999/2000	1,500

The Revenue may argue that the correct terminal loss should be computed by taking the loss for the year ended 31 December 2000 after relief under *s 385*. This would then give a loss unrelieved for that year of £1,500, restricting the terminal loss relief to £750. The legislation is ambiguous, and the interpretation of *ICTA 1988, s 388(2)* shown in the example above is more favourable to the taxpayer.

Restriction of relief in respect of farming and market gardening

11.21 The additional restrictions in *ICTA 1988, s 397* continue to apply to ensure that loss relief will only be granted to farmers and market gardeners where the business has made a profit in at least one of the preceding five years (unless a competent farmer or market gardener could not have expected a profit).

This restriction applied where there was not an adjusted profit before capital allowances. With the introduction of the treatment of capital allowances as a trading expense, this would have altered the test under *s 397*. It is therefore provided that in carrying out the test under *s 397* the profit shall be computed without regard to capital allowances, thus keeping the previous test intact.

Relief for losses on unquoted shares

11.22 When an individual had subscribed for shares in a qualifying trading company and those shares have resulted in an allowable loss for capital gains tax purposes, then it is possible for the taxpayer to elect to treat the loss as being an income tax loss [*ICTA 1988, s 574*].

With effect from 1994/95, relief under this section will be given against other income for the year of loss. Alternatively the taxpayer may elect for relief against other income for the year preceding the year of loss.

Where a claim is made for relief in the current year, then a further claim can be made for any balance of the loss to be given against general income of the preceding year [new *ICTA 1988, s 574(1)(2)* substituted by *FA 1994, s 210*].

The time limit for claiming relief under *s 574* remains as two years from the end of the tax year in which the loss was incurred for the years 1994/95 and 1995/96 [*FA 1994, 20 Sch 8*]. From 1996/97, the time limit will be twelve months from 31 January following the year of loss.

Loss relief in 1996/97

11.23 Because loss relief under the previous rules was given on a fiscal year basis, whereas assessments were calculated on a preceding year basis, there was not normally a duplication of losses in opening year aggregation. Accordingly, loss relief is not included in the calculation of the transitional year assessment. Trading losses available for 1996/97 will be given in full against the taxpayer's general income for that year or the year preceding (1995/96), with any unused losses being available for carry forward against subsequent profits of the same trade.

It would appear that the transitional assessment will be calculated by reference to the profits of the transitional period and then any *s 385* loss relief brought forward will be deducted from the resultant assessable profits. In the same way, losses arising during the basis period for the transitional year will not be restricted, but will be available for carry forward in full under *s 385*.

11.24 *Losses*

Example

11.24 John Smith, who makes up his accounts to 31 December for many years, has the following adjusted profits and capital allowances. He is single and has other income of £5,000 per year. (Fiscal year basis of loss claim does not apply.)

	Profit before capital allowances	Capital allowances
	£	£
Year ended 31.12.94	7,000	1,450
31.12.95	2,100	600
31.12.96	(10,000)	
31.12.97	6,000	450

Assessments with claim for *s 380* loss relief:

		£	£
1996/97	Year ended 31.12.95	2,100	
	Year ended 31.12.96	NIL	

	£	£
365/731 x 2,100		1,048
Less capital allowances		600
		448
Other income		5,000
		5,448
Less s 380 loss		5,448
		NIL

S 380 loss relief 1996/97:

Loss year ended 31 December 1996		10,000
Available:		
Year of loss 1996/97	5,448	
Year preceding 1995/96	4,552	10,000

1995/96		
Schedule D I Profits	7,000	
Less capital allowances	1,450	5,550
Other income		5,000
		10,550
Less s 380 loss		4,552
		5,998
Less personal allowance		3,525
		2,473

S 380 relief could have been claimed for the preceding year only. This will give a better result:

Losses **11.24**

Loss available in 1995/96 – £10,000

	£
1996/97 as above	5,448
Less personal allowances (say)	3,525
	1,923
1995/96 – as above	10,550
Less s 380 relief	10,000
	550
Less personal allowance	550
	NIL

The amount on which tax is payable is therefore reduced from £2,473 in 1995/96 to £1,923 in 1996/97.

Alternatively, relief could be claimed under *s 385* giving assessable amounts of:

	£	£
1996/97 – Schedule D I (as above)		448
Other income		5,000
		5,448
Less personal allowance		3,525
		1,923
1997/98 – Schedule D I	5,550	
Less loss b/f	10,000	
Loss c/f under *s 385*	4,450	NIL
Other income		5,000
Less personal allowance		3,525
		1,475

This would leave £4,450 relievable against Schedule D I profits after capital allowances of the year ended 31 December 1998 and subsequent years, which may be the best possible alternative dependant upon the total taxable income of 1998/99 and the tax rates in each year.

Chapter 12

Other Changes

Principles of self-assessment

12.1 The introduction of self-assessment and the current year basis will have a far-reaching effect on the way all taxes are assessed and collected.

The basic principle of calculating the liability to tax by reference to the rules of a schedule continues to apply. Having arrived at the quantum of the assessable income then those amounts are aggregated to form one self-assessment.

Because the taxpayer is making one self-assessment, he will only deal with one tax office and he will only have one tax reference. That reference will be different to any partnership reference.

12.2 In the case of partnerships, the partnership return and statement will be forwarded to the partnership tax district to agree the liability. The resultant division of income from all sources will be on the basis of the profit-sharing ratio of the period of account.

Accordingly, having arrived at the income chargeable under Schedule D Case III, etc. for the period of account, this is divided between the partners in the profit-sharing ratio for the accounting period. Effectively, therefore, a different basis arises when Schedule D Case III income is received by a partnership compared with the receipt of the same income by an individual.

The same applies to all income received by the partnership, e.g. Schedule D Case I or II, Schedule A lettings, Schedule D Case VI furnished lettings or Schedule D Case IV and V overseas income.

Schedule D Case III

12.3 The basis of assessment under Schedule D Case III changes from the preceding year basis (in most instances) to an actual basis on all occasions [new *ICTA 1988, s 64* substituted by *FA 1994, s 206*]. As with trading income, the provisions apply to new sources from 6 April 1994. In the case of existing sources, the old rules apply if the source ceases before 6 April 1998 [*FA 1994, 20 Sch 5*].

12.4 In the case of continuing sources, that is to say, where the income arose before 6 April 1994 and continues beyond 5 April 1998, then:

(a) the old rules apply for 1994/95 and 1995/96 (preceding year basis);
(b) for 1996/97, the assessment will be one half of the interest received in 1995/96 and 1996/97 [*FA 1994, 20 Sch 4(2)*]; and
(c) for 1997/98 and subsequent years, the income actually arising in the fiscal year will form the basis of assessment.

It must be remembered that if the old rules apply and there is a cessation, then the Revenue have the option to revise the penultimate assessment to actual.

Example of a continuing source

12.5 Henry Ing has received bank deposit interest for many years. His interest received is:

		£
Year ended	5 April 1995	1,800
	5 April 1996	1,750
	5 April 1997	1,650
	5 April 1998	1,500

His income assessable under Schedule D III is:

	£
1995/96 (preceding year basis)	1,800
1996/97 (transitional year)	
Year ended 5.4.96 1,750	
Year ended 5.4.97 <u>1,650</u>	
50% x <u>3,400</u>	1,700
1997/98 (actual)	1,500

Example of a source closing before 5 April 1998

12.6 Henry closes his deposit account on 31 December 1997, with interest for that part year of £1,500.

His assessable Schedule D III income would be:

	£
1995/96 (preceding year basis)	1,800
1996/97 (preceding year basis)	1,750
(with Revenue option to revise to actual - £1,650)	
1997/98 (actual)	1,500

(The transitional year (1996/97) only applies if the source continues beyond 5 April 1998).

Example of a new source

12.7 Ingrid James opened a National Savings investment account in June 1994.

12.8 Other Changes

Her income from that account was:

	£
Year ended 5 April 1995	1,800
5 April 1996	1,750
5 April 1997	1,650
5 April 1998	1,500

Her Schedule D III assessments are all on an actual basis:

	£
1994/95	1,800
1995/96	1,750
1996/97	1,650
1997/98	1,500

Schedule D Cases IV and V

12.8 Similar rules apply to overseas income as to UK income. If the source is a foreign trade, profession or vocation chargeable to tax under Schedule D Case IV or Case V, it is to be assessed as though it were a Schedule D Case I source. That is to say, in future years the current year basis of assessment will apply, with transitional rules for 1996/97 and overlap relief as for Schedule D Cases I and II.

Other sources of Schedule D Case IV and Case V income are to be treated as for Schedule D Case III above, that is to say on an actual basis providing the source continues beyond 5 April 1998 [*FA 1994, s 207, 20 Sch 6,7*].

12.9 Summary of basis of assessment

If source arises before 6 April 1994 and continues beyond 5 April 1998	Actual basis applies for 1997/98 onwards
	Transitional rules apply for 1996/97, that is one half of the income arising in 1995/96 and 1996/97
	Preceding year basis applies up to and including 1995/96. If 1995/96 is on actual basis, then actual will apply throughout.
If source commences after 5 April 1994	New rules apply 1994 immediately (actual basis)
If source ceases before 6 April 1998 and had commenced before 6 April 1994	Preceding year basis rules apply throughout

Remittance basis

12.10 Because the remittance basis may apply to Schedule D Cases IV and V, anti-avoidance provisions have been introduced in the *Finance Act 1995* to prevent exceptionally large remittances being made during the transitional period. Without such provisions, it would have been possible to make large remittances during the period 6 April 1995 to 5 April 1997 and only 50% thereof would be taxed.

The anti-avoidance rules have the same effect as those for Schedule D, Cases I and II, which are set out at 7.9 above.

Other income assessable under Schedule D, Cases IV and V will, in addition to being assessed in the normal way, be subject to what is in effect a 'penalty assessment' on 12.5% of the amount artificially shifted into the yeas 1995/96 and 1996/97 by means of relevant arrangements or transactions (subject to de minimis limits to be announced) [*FA 1995, 22 Sch 10*].

'Relevant arrangements' will be any arrangements under which income arises at irregular intervals, unless they are exclusively made for bona fide commercial reasons, or the obtaining of a tax advantage is not the main benefit that could reasonably be expected to arise [*FA 1995, 22 Sch 19*].

'Relevant transactions' are any transactions with an associated person, unless they are exclusively for bona fide commercial reasons, or the obtaining of a tax advantage is not the main benefit that could reasonably be expected to arise [*FA 1995, 22 Sch 20*].

For the purpose of these rules, if the assessment is based upon the remittance basis, then the source is treated as arising on the date on which the first amount of income is received in the UK.

Schedule D Case VI

12.11 Income tax under Schedule D Case VI will be computed on the full amount of profits or gains arising in the year of assessment [new I*CTA, 1988, s 69* substituted by *FA 1994, s 208*]. This applies immediately to sources of Schedule D Case VI income arising on or after 6 April 1994 and to existing sources with effect from 1996/97.

In practice, Schedule D Case VI is often dealt with on an accounts basis or even on a preceding year basis. It is expected that the Revenue will allow a current year basis to apply in the future to those sources already dealt with on that basis. This will apply automatically to partnerships.

In the case of Schedule D Case VI currently being assessed on a preceding year basis, it is expected that transitional provisions will apply for 1996/97 by taking 50% of the income that would have been assessed for that year on the preceding year basis plus the current year basis.

12.12 Other Changes

Although there are no statutory provisions available, it should be suggested to the Revenue that overlap relief should apply as for trades, professions and vocations.

Lloyd's underwriters

12.12 Where the first underwriting year for a member of Lloyd's is the year 1994 then, although they will become a member from 1 January 1994, they are deemed to have commenced on 6 April 1994.

For all individual members, the results of the calendar year 1994 will be assessed in 1997/98, i.e. the calendar year in which the results are declared. Accordingly, a new underwriter would use self-assessment for their results from commencement on or after 1 January 1994.

For existing underwriters, basic rate tax on the 1992 account will be due on 1 January 1996 and higher rate tax on 31 January 1997. For year of account 1993, basic rate tax will be due on 1 January 1997 and higher rate tax on 31 January 1998.

Thereafter, tax will be due under self-assessment and will be included in the normal payments due on 31 January in the year and 31 July following the year of assessment. Therefore, for the accounts year 1994, tax will initially be due on 31 January 1998 and 31 July 1998, with any balancing payment due or repayable on 31 January 1999.

If losses arise, the Revenue will give effect to a claim for loss relief as soon as the figures are available.

Double taxation relief in respect of overlap profits

12.13 Rules are introduced for allocating double taxation relief in respect of overlap profits, to broadly ensure that all relief available for foreign tax is given over the lifetime of the business.

Relief is given in the opening years against the amounts assessed twice. On cessation any excess credit has to be determined, being the difference between the credit allowed when the overlap profit was created and the credit that would have been available had the income only be assessed once. The difference is then set off against the credit that would have been allowed in the year of clawback had profits not been restricted by overlap relief. If excess credit has been given, the excess is recovered by way of a Schedule D Case VI charge at the basic rate, such that the tax due equals the excess credit. If insufficient credit has been allowed, a further credit is available in the latter year.

Similar rules apply on a change of accounting date, that is to say additional overlap relief may be created or withdrawn, giving rise to double relief or withdrawal as in opening and closing years [*FA 1994, s 217*].

Farmers' averaging provisions

12.14 Farmers' profit averaging provisions, under *ICTA 1988, s 96*, continue to apply under the new rules. However, previously the provisions applied to the profits before capital allowances. From 1997/98, capital allowances become a deduction as a trading expense and, accordingly, in future the averaging will be undertaken with profits after capital allowances.

The new rules will apply for businesses commencing on or after 6 April 1994 immediately. For existing businesses, i.e. those that commenced before 6 April 1994 and continue after 6 April 1997, averaging will take place before capital allowances for the years 1995/96 and 1996/97.

Where the average is to be applied to the years 1996/97 and 1997/98, or any later years, averaging will be under the new rules, i.e. after capital allowances.

In the case of partnerships, the averaging up to and including 1995/96 and 1996/97 will be made by reference to the partnership. Thereafter, i.e. for averaging for 1996/97 and 1997/98 or subsequent years, the claim and calculation will be made by the individual partner. For partnerships commencing or deemed to have commenced on or after 6 April 1994, all claims will be on an individual basis.

Schedule E

12.15 Schedule E is computed on amounts paid on a fiscal year basis. Therefore, no changes are necessary to bring Schedule E income in line with self-assessment rules. Nevertheless, there will be a consequential effect upon Schedule E of the change from Revenue assessment to self-assessment.

12.16 When completing a tax return, it will be essential to include figures of income chargeable for the fiscal year and to know the tax deducted at source. Accordingly, it will be essential to have sight of form P60 or equivalent. To include the relevant income from benefits, it will be necessary to incorporate within the tax return the amounts assessable on form P11D or form P9D. A claim for expenses under *ICTA 1988, s 198*, etc. must be incorporated within the tax return in order to compute the self-assessed income. Accordingly, where the amount exceeds £1,000, underpayments by way of the PAYE system will not be adjusted by the Revenue or collected by assessment issued by the Revenue. Instead they will form part of the self-assessment and will be paid automatically by the taxpayer on 31 January following the year of assessment.

Great care will be needed to ensure that the tax paid (as shown on form P60) relates wholly to the fiscal year of assessment. If there has been a coding adjustment to collect underpaid Schedule E in earlier years, then that amount of tax must be deducted from the tax paid under PAYE for the year to arrive at the amount to be included within the self-assessment.

12.17 The effect of the above changes will be that, where a tax return has been issued, the Schedule E taxpayer must return the form by 30 September

12.18 *Other Changes*

including full details of income and benefits, in order for the Revenue to assess the taxpayer. Therefore, it is essential that employers meet the new deadline of 6 July for completion of forms P11D and P9D and provide copies of the forms to employees. Form P60 must be given to an employee by 31 May.

12.18 A further complication arises in respect of expenses received by an employee which are covered by special arrangements, e.g. dispensations, Fixed Profit Car Scheme arrangements or working rule arrangements. Employees must be made aware of the need to exclude such figures from their personal tax returns, but to include any other expense payments.

12.19 Where a tax return has been issued, interest will automatically arise on Schedule E underpayments with effect from 31 January following the end of the year of assessment. Furthermore, surcharges could apply, and an automatic penalty will apply for failure to file a completed tax return by the due date. The Revenue will take the view that the submission of a tax return with the words 'as returned' or 'as per P60' shown thereon would be the submission of an incomplete return, giving rise to a penalty.

Capital gains

12.20 The taxpayer must include computations of capital gains and capital losses within the tax return. Any capital gains tax payable will be due on 31 January following the end of the year of assessment. Under self-assessment the taxpayer must make a claim for capital losses within the tax return. If a claim is not made then loss relief will not be granted. *FA 1995, s 113* provides that losses of 1996/97 and subsequent years are to be deductible from capital gains in preference to capital losses of earlier years brought forward.

In computing a capital gain or capital loss it is necessary in many instances to use a valuation. Valuations necessarily require the exercise of judgement, and more than one figure may equally be sustainable. The basis of valuation should be shown in the tax return. If the taxpayer believes that the valuation is a considered figure then it will be regarded as the final figure subject to the Revenue's right to enquire into the tax return. If the Revenue do not enquire into a valuation figure within the normal enquiry period, i.e. within twelve months of 31 January following the end of the year of assessment (or later if the return is filed later), then it cannot challenge that valuation at a later date unless it is 'unreasonable'.

If the taxpayer believes that the figure is an estimate then it should be shown as such on the return and the figure should be corrected as soon as any missing information is reasonably available.

The Inland Revenue intend to issue a more detailed statement on estimates and valuations before 1997.

Future legislation

12.21 The Inland Revenue is currently undertaking further consultation with

Other Changes **12.21**

interested parties and this will result in further legislation, to be included in the *Finance Act 1996,* in respect of self-assessment and the current year basis.

It is to be expected that there will be numerous changes to detailed points relating to self-assessment and the current year basis in many of the forthcoming Finance Bills. As many provisions do not come into force until 1996/97 or 1997/98, it is essential to refer to such legislation when available before giving definitive advice.

Index

A

Accounting date, change of,	**9**
accounts for more than 18 months,	9.12, 9.13
conditions for change,	9.6, 9.7
failure to give notice,	9.14
objectives of legislation,	9.1
transitional period, in,	7.6–7.8
whether worthwhile,	7.10–7.13
Administration,	2.4–2.13
Amendments to self-assessments,	2.42
Anti-avoidance provisions,	7.9
Apportionments,	6.4
Assessments,	
current year basis,	**5**
—concepts,	5.8–5.10
—dealings with Inland Revenue,	5.17, 5.18
—new rules,	5.11–5.16
discovery,	2.11
1995/96 and earlier years,	3.29
opening and closing years,	**6**
—accounts prepared to 5 April,	6.6, 6.7, 6.26, 6.27
—apportionments,	6.4
—capital allowances and losses,	6.3
—commencement of new rules,	6.23
—first accounts,	6.13–6.22
—overlap relief,	6.2
—short-life businesses,	6.12
—use of 31 March as year end,	6.5
transitional rules,	**7**

C

Capital allowances,	**8**
claims for,	8.4
deduction as a trading expense,	8.2
introduction of new rules,	8.6, 8.7
notification of expenditure,	8.5
opening and closing years,	6.3
period of account,	8.3
Capital gains,	12.20
Claims,	3.26
error or mistake,	3.27, 3.28
Closing years,	**6**
accounts prepared to 5 April,	6.26, 6.27
apportionments,	6.4
capital allowances and losses,	6.3
existing businesses ceasing,	6.34–6.39
overlap relief,	6.2, 6.25
use of 31 March as year end,	6.5
Current year basis of assessment,	**5**
concepts,	5.8–5.10
dealings with Inland Revenue,	5.17, 5.18
new rules,	5.11–5.16
partnerships,	10.15–10.17

D

Determinations, where no return delivered,	3.15, 3.16
Discovery,	2.11, 3.17, 3.18
Documents,	
failure to produce,	3.24
power to call for,	2.41
Double taxation relief, overlap profits,	12.13

E

Error or mistake claims, 3.27, 3.28

F

Farming,	
averaging provisions,	12.14
restriction of loss relief,	11.21
Future legislation,	12.21

Index

H

Higher rate liability, payment of tax for 1996/97,	4.3

I

Inland Revenue, dealings with,	5.17, 5.18
Interest,	3.2–3.10
penalties, on,	3.25

L

Lloyd's underwriters,	12.12
Losses,	**11**
carried forward,	11.15, 11.16
current year basis,	11.3–11.6
farming and market gardening, restriction of relief,	11.21
fiscal year basis in practice,	11.1, 11.2
national insurance, relief for,	11.14
opening years, relief in,	11.11–11.13
other income, relief against,	11.7–11.10
relief in 1996/97,	11.23, 11.24
terminal,	11.17–11.20
unquoted shares, relief for losses on,	11.22

M

March 31, used as year-end,	6.5
Market gardening, restriction of loss relief,	11.21

N

Notification of sources of income,	2.16–2.19

O

Opening years,	**6**
accounts prepared to 5 April,	6.6, 6.7
apportionments,	6.4
capital allowances and losses,	6.3
commencement of new rules,	6.23
first accounts,	6.13–6.22
overlap relief,	6.2
short-life businesses,	6.12
summary of rules,	6.24
use of 31 March as year end,	6.5
Overlap profits, double taxation relief,	12.13
Overlap relief,	6.2, 6.25
existing businesses,	7.3, 7.4

P

Partnerships,	**10**
assessed on actual basis in 1995/96,	10.18, 10.20
change of partner before 5 April 1997,	10.12
continuing partners,	10.11
corporate partners,	10.21
current year basis,	10.15–10.17
income other than Schedule D Case I or II,	10.22
new partners,	10.6–10.8
payment of tax for 1996/97,	4.10
retirement of a partner,	10.9, 10.10
returns,	2.24–2.30
self-assessment with partnership income,	10.1–10.5
statements,	2.28, 2.29
transitional period,	10.13, 10.14
Payment,	
date of,	2.4–2.6, 2.46–2.52
1996/97,	**4**
—computation of amount payable,	4.7
—higher rate liability,	4.3
—partnerships,	4.10

Index

—payments on
   account,   4.1, 4.2, 4.6
—Schedule A,   4.4
—Schedule D Cases I
   and II,   4.5, 4.8
—Schedule D Cases III–VI,   4.4
Penalties,   3
  documents, failure to
    produce,   3.24
  failure to notify
    chargeability,   3.21, 3.22
  interest on,   3.25
  late returns,   3.19, 3.20
  records, failure to keep,   3.23

R

Records,   2.20–2.23
  penalties for failure to keep, 3.23
Returns,   2.14
  corrections to,   2.8
  enquiries into,   2.9, 2.32–2.45
  filing dates,   2.15
  partnership,   2.24–2.30
  trustees,   2.31

S

Schedule A, payment of tax
  for 1996/97,   4.4
Schedule D Cases I and II,
  payment of tax for
  1996/97,   4.5, 4.8
Schedule D Case III,
  basis of assessment,   12.3–12.7
  payment of tax for 1996/97,   4.4
Schedule D Cases IV–V,
  basis of assessment,   12.8, 12.9
  payment of tax for 1996/97,   4.4
  remittance basis,   12.10
Schedule D Case VI,
  basis of assessment,   12.11
  payment of tax for 1996/97,   4.4
Schedule E,   12.15–12.20
Short-life businesses,   6.12
Surcharges,   3.11–3.13

T

Tax districts,   2.12
Time limits,   2.13
Transitional rules for existing
  businesses,   7
  accounting date, whether
    change worthwhile, 7.10–7.13
  anti-avoidance provisions,   7.9
  businesses not on PY basis
    for 1995/96,   7.14, 7.15
  change of accounting date
    in transitional period,   7.6–7.8
  overlap relief,   7.3, 7.4
  partnerships,   10.13, 10.14
Trustees,   2.31

U

Underwriters,   12.12